Published by Place Forward Strategies, LLC, a subsidiary of Martin Sisters Publishing Company, Inc.

ISBN: 978-1-62553-117-9

Published in the United States by Place Forward Strategies, LLC.

Kentucky

CONTENTS

About the book

Story & Place: Journalism Training Course for Community Correspondents is designed as the central learning resource for students, emerging reporters, and community communicators enrolled in the Community News Correspondent Training Program. Built from the combined foundations of teaching hundreds of journalism students everything from media law to feature writing, editing, and quoting sources, and real-world reporting practice, this textbook serves as a structured, practical, and deeply contextual guide to understanding how journalism operates at the local level.

While many journalism textbooks focus on national newsrooms and metropolitan case studies, this companion book takes a different path. It begins with the understanding that place matters, and that communities require reporting approaches that respect cultural nuance, historical context, and the lived realities of people whose stories are too often simplified or overlooked. Whether you're covering a school board dispute, a public health challenge, a natural disaster, or a community celebration, strong journalism grows from understanding the people behind the issues, their stakes, their struggles, and the systems that shape their lives.

This Textbook breaks down the craft of reporting into clear, accessible chapters that guide readers through story discovery, interviewing, narrative structure, verification, breaking-news discipline, editing, and ethical decision-making. Each chapter blends practical instruction with real-world examples, case studies, exercises, and reflective prompts to help students develop not just technical skill, but journalistic judgment, the ability to choose stories responsibly, frame them ethically, and produce work that strengthens community trust.

Designed as a companion to the online classroom modules and in-field assignments, this book can be used alongside weekly lessons or as a standalone reference. It supports learners in developing the full reporting process: from idea to final draft, from quick updates to long-form stories, from interviewing everyday residents to analyzing institutional power. Most importantly, it prepares journalists to work with integrity, humility, and a deep understanding of the communities they serve.

Whether you're new to reporting or enhancing what you already know, *Story & Place: Community Correspondent Journalism Training* will help you build the skills, awareness, and confidence to tell stories that matter, rooted in context, character, fairness and truth.

CHAPTER 1

REASON FOR THE STORY

PLACED-BASED LEARNING SERIES

Section 1.1: What Makes a Good Story?

Anecdote: The Story That Didn't Land

Maria, a first-semester journalism student, rushed into the newsroom one Friday with what she believed was a great scoop. She had spent the entire evening carefully documenting every line of a seemingly important city council decision: the approval of new snowplows. She captured the vote tally, contract price, and delivery timeline with precision. When she filed her story, "The council approved a $250,000 purchase of snowplows on Thursday night by a vote of 6–1", she felt satisfied. Her facts were solid. The meeting was covered. The story was, in her mind, complete.

Her editor leaned back in his chair and asked the question no reporter wants to hear: **"So what?"**

Maria hadn't expected that. She knew the number, knew the facts, knew the procedural details. But what she did not yet understand was that journalism is not driven by process alone. It is driven by impact.

When she returned to the neighborhood to speak with residents, the story changed dramatically. A mother described how her street remained snowed in for two consecutive winters, delaying ambulances and putting lives at risk. A small business owner explained how delayed snow clearing kept customers away, costing him thousands in revenue. In those voices, Maria found what her earlier draft had completely missed: the stakes. The human consequences. The lived reality behind the vote.

> The snowplow contract wasn't about municipal spending. It was about safety, mobility, and survival. Once framed this way, it became a story that mattered.

If your story can't pass the 'So what?' test, it won't matter to your audience.

Concept: What Makes a Story "Good"?

A good story does not start with information; it starts with meaning. It must answer two instinctive questions every editor, reader, and audience member brings to news:

"So what?" Why does this matter? What is at stake? What changes because this happened?

"Only here." Why does this story belong uniquely to this community, this moment, or this publication?

These two questions form the foundation of news judgment. A story that fails either one may be factual but irrelevant; accurate but uninteresting; complete but lacking significance.

This is where classic news values come in. They function not as a checklist, but as a set of lenses that help journalists understand which stories deserve attention and why. Terms like impact, timeliness, proximity, prominence, conflict, novelty, and human interest are not abstract, they are tools that help determine how deeply a story will resonate with the public. A good story usually shines strongly through one or two of these values and uses them to anchor its narrative.

Classic News Values: The Foundation of Strong Storytelling

Impact, at its core, measures how people's lives are changed. A decision, event, or discovery with significant consequences for a large number of people naturally demands coverage. Timeliness reminds us that news is about the present moment; the closer an event is to "now," the more urgent it becomes. Proximity ties the story to the community's daily lived experience; an issue that happens locally or affects neighbors carries more emotional weight. Prominence involves public figures whose actions have a broad influence. Conflict reveals the tensions that make stories dramatic and meaningful. Novelty captures what is unexpected, surprising, or emotionally gripping. And human interest connects readers through empathy and relatability.

These values overlap constantly. A story does not need all of them, but it must clearly excel in at least one.

Real-World Examples: When News Values Work, and When They Fail

The Flint Water Crisis stands as one of the most powerful examples of high-impact reporting in recent years. When The Washington Post covered Flint, its stories resonated because they did far more than list facts. They centered on parents whose children became sick, highlighted official misconduct, and provided continuous updates as new evidence emerged. The combination of impact, conflict, proximity, and human interest turned a local crisis into a national reckoning.

Contrast this with Hurricane Katrina's early coverage. Many national outlets failed to contextualize suffering within systemic racism and governmental failure. Instead, they leaned heavily on novelty and sensationalism, labelling Black survivors as "looters" while describing white survivors as people "finding" food. This disparity became a case study in how misuse of news values can reinforce harmful stereotypes and erode trust.

A more localized example comes from Appalachia, where The Charleston Gazette-Mail's opioid crisis reporting is now widely studied. The journalists succeeded because they didn't rely on clichés about addiction. They layered impact (overdose rates), conflict (legal battles against drug distributors), and human interest (families stepping into caregiving roles) to create a story that was both intimate and nationally relevant.

> Stories succeed or fail depending on how news values are used, not just whether they appear.

News values aren't checkboxes; they are lenses.

Craft Guidance: Applying News Values in Real Reporting

In practice, reporters start with fragments: a rumor, a tip, a document, a trend, a meeting note. These are raw ingredients, not yet stories. To shape them into journalism, the reporter first applies the "So what?" test. Can the stakes be explained clearly in a single sentence? If not, more reporting is needed.

Next comes the "Only here" test. A generic issue becomes distinctive when tied to local decisions, local people, or local consequences. A national trend becomes meaningful when traced to how it touches a specific community.

Then the journalist determines which news values are strongest. A story with weak impact but strong novelty may belong as a feature. A story with strong conflict and timeliness may work as breaking news. A story centered on human interest may be best told as a profile.

> Choosing the correct form, whether inverted pyramid, hourglass, narrative arc, or Q&A, ensures the structure matches the story's purpose.

Cross-Cultural Context: When News Values Become Harmful

News values can also cause distortion. Novelty has been misused to exoticize Indigenous communities, turning cultural practices into spectacle. Conflict has been narrowly applied to immigrant neighborhoods reducing them to violence-filled caricatures. Human interest can slip into poverty voyeurism when suffering is displayed without context or dignity.

These are not minor missteps; they shape public perception.

Reporters must learn that news values are powerful but ethically sensitive tools. They must be used with care, context, and cultural awareness.

Strengthening Story Judgment: Narrative Instead of Bullets

A strong story idea emerges through a series of questions, not through a checklist:

You begin by asking whether the issue touches real people in significant ways. Then you consider whether something new has happened to make the story urgent. You think about proximity, how close this event is to the daily routines of your community. You identify the people at the center of the story and ask what conflict they face, what decisions they are navigating, and what consequences lie ahead. You then reflect on whether the story has an ending, clear resolution or a truthful moment of uncertainty.

> A story becomes clearer as these questions sharpen. The more precisely a reporter can answer them, the stronger the story becomes.

Pitfalls That Weaken Story Ideas

A story often falters not because it lacks information, but because it lacks coherence. Many emerging journalists fall into the trap of "laundry-list coverage", piling facts, quotes, and details without guiding readers toward a central meaning. Others rely too heavily on official voices, leaving ordinary people invisible. Some chase novelty simply because it is unusual, even when it lacks significance. Others frame conflict in exaggerated ways that create drama but distort reality. And sometimes journalists imply resolution where none exists, misleading readers into believing an issue is solved.

A story often falters not because it lacks information, but because it lacks coherence

These pitfalls are common, but avoidable with stronger story judgment.

Reflection Activity: Turning Tips into Real Stories

Consider three everyday community events: a traffic light installed downtown, a high school sports victory, and a county proposal to reduce library hours. Each one could be a dull announcement or a meaningful narrative. The difference lies in how the reporter approaches it.

If the new traffic light reduces accidents at a dangerous intersection, the story becomes public safety. If the sports victory represents a historic first for a school or a moment of pride for families, it becomes human interest. If library cuts affect children, job seekers, or elderly residents, the story becomes about equity and access.

The power of a story is rarely in the event; it is in the stakes behind it.

Case Study: *Snow Fall*, The Avalanche at Tunnel Creek

The New York Times' 2012 feature *Snow Fall* remains a landmark example of long-form digital storytelling. Although it gained attention for its multimedia design, its real strength came from fundamental reporting choices: clear characters, layered conflict, and an honest resolution.

The narrative begins not with exposition, but with people, skiers moving through snow, anticipating adventure. When the avalanche hits, the conflict extends beyond the mountain itself, encompassing human risk-taking, environmental conditions, and emotional aftermath. The resolution does not pretend that tragedy is solved; it acknowledges the consequences and the lessons learned.

This case demonstrates that technology enhances storytelling but cannot replace craft.

Key Takeaways

A strong story is built from clarity, relevance, and human significance. News values guide story selection, but only when used responsibly. Characters carry meaning; conflict creates stakes; resolution, even when incomplete, provides closure. And storytelling must avoid stereotypes, distortions, and spectacle.

A good story, at its core, is one that helps people understand their world.

Section 1.2: News Values in Depth

News values are the heartbeat of journalism. They determine which stories rise to the top of a newsroom meeting and which ones fade into the background. While Section 1.1 introduced these values broadly, this section digs deeper into how they operate in real-world reporting, why they matter, and how journalists can apply them with nuance and sensitivity. Understanding news values at a surface level is easy; understanding how they intersect with culture, community, and storytelling complexity is what sets strong journalists apart.

At their core, news values are a way of measuring significance. They help reporters answer the question, "Is this important enough to become news?" But they are also a way of shaping public awareness, what audiences think about, what they pay attention to, and what they perceive as meaningful. Because of that influence, news values carry both power and responsibility. They give structure to storytelling, but they also have the potential to distort reality when used carelessly or without context.

Impact: The Weight of Consequences

Impact asks how deeply an issue affects people's lives. A decision that changes a family's access to healthcare or a policy that shifts how thousands of residents experience public safety automatically carries weight. But impact is not only measured by the number of people affected; it is also measured by how profoundly lives are changed. A story about one person wrongfully imprisoned may have more emotional and moral weight than a story about a minor inconvenience faced by thousands.

> Understanding impact requires journalists to think beyond statistics. It requires them to locate real lives inside the data and to understand how consequences ripple beyond the immediate moment. Good reporters learn to ask: Who is touched by this? Who is vulnerable? Who benefits? And who is placed at risk if this story remains untold?

Timeliness: Why It Matters *Now*

Timeliness is often misunderstood as simply reporting something quickly. In reality, timeliness is about relevance. A story becomes newsworthy because something has changed or new evidence has emerged, a decision has been made, a deadline has arrived, or a crisis has intensified. Timeliness introduces urgency, but it does not negate depth. A timely story must still be accurate and grounded, even when pressure to publish quickly increases.

A story becomes newsworthy because something has changed or new evidence has emerged, a decision has been made, a deadline has arrived, or a crisis has intensified.

Timeliness also interacts with community rhythms. A weather emergency feels urgent in one region; a political development feels urgent in another. Journalists must stay attuned to what matters right now in the community they serve.

Proximity: The Power of Local Connection

Proximity reminds us that news is, above all, local. An issue happening across the country may carry national implications, but people naturally prioritize what shapes *their* streets, *their* schools, *their* hospitals, and *their* daily routines. When a national trend, like rising rent, affordable housing shortages, or changes in healthcare access—lands in a local community, it gains new resonance.

Strong journalists know how to "localize" broader issues. They connect national policies to neighborhood consequences, introduce audiences to local people navigating big challenges, and show how everyday life intersects with larger forces. Proximity is what transforms abstract issues into relatable narratives.

Prominence: When People and Institutions Drive a Story

Prominence does not automatically make a story important, but it does raise its stakes. When a governor makes a statement, a school board faces controversy, or a well-known business leader announces a decision, the public pays closer attention because these individuals or institutions have influence. But prominence must be handled carefully; it should not overshadow the lived experiences of ordinary people. A mayor's decision is newsworthy not because the mayor is important, but because their power affects others.

> Editors teach reporters to understand prominence as a value that must always be paired with impact. The most meaningful stories center the people who feel the consequences, not just those who wield authority.

Conflict: The Engine of Narrative

Conflict gives stories tension, movement, and purpose. It is not limited to arguments or hostility; conflict appears whenever there is struggle, uncertainty, tension, or competing interests. A debate over school funding is in conflict. A community navigating water shortages is in conflict. A neighborhood pushing back against redevelopment is in conflict.

Strong reporters show conflict as layered rather than one-dimensional. They dig into the historical tensions, systemic forces, and personal stakes behind a disagreement. They show how individuals navigate conflicting responsibilities and values. Conflict becomes a lens through which deeper truths are revealed.

Novelty & Human Interest: The Unexpected and the Emotional

Novelty captures what is unusual, surprising, or visually compelling. A fish falling from the sky during a storm. A goat wandering into a courthouse. A man building a tiny library out of recycled materials. These moments get attention because they break the pattern of everyday life, yet novelty becomes journalism only when paired with context. Otherwise, it becomes a spectacle.

Human interest taps into empathy and relatability. It asks readers to connect emotionally with someone else's experience. These stories highlight the resilience of a single mother navigating hardship, the dedication of a teacher shaping young lives, or the quiet determination of a farmer working through drought.

> Human interest brings warmth; novelty brings surprise. But both require responsibility. Journalists must avoid exploiting vulnerability or turning communities into curiosity pieces. Without care, these values can slip into stereotype or tokenism.

Using News Values with Intention

One of the biggest lessons for emerging journalists is that news values require interpretation, not blind application. A story does not become meaningful simply because it is unusual or timely. A story becomes meaningful when news values are used to illuminate real stakes, clarify complexity, and elevate voices that matter.

A story does not become meaningful simply because it is unusual or timely.

This requires judgment: the ability to weigh context, understand community priorities, and anticipate how readers will interpret the story. It requires sensitivity: the ability to recognize when novelty slips into stereotype, when conflict becomes sensationalized, and when human interest turns exploitative. And it requires humility: the understanding that news values can mislead if used without cultural awareness.

News values, when applied with thoughtfulness, help journalists build stories that matter, not just stories that grab attention.

Section 1.3: Characters, Conflict & Stakes: The Human Engine of Storytelling

Journalism begins with facts, but it comes alive through people. No matter how significant a policy, statistic, or trend may be, audiences understand it most clearly through the individuals who live its consequences. Characters provide an entry point into complexity. They turn abstract issues into relatable experiences, and they give stories the emotional gravity needed to hold attention. In this way, characters are not decorative additions to a story; they are the primary carriers of meaning.

No matter how significant a policy, statistic, or trend may be, audiences understand it most clearly through the individuals who live its consequences.

Why Characters Matter

Characters allow readers to interpret information through a human lens. When a journalist introduces a person with clear stakes, someone facing a challenge, navigating uncertainty, or experiencing the weight of a decision, readers begin to care. They listen differently. They absorb more deeply. The human brain is wired to understand the world through narrative, and narrative is almost impossible without people.

This does not mean every story requires dramatic personalities. A "character" in journalism can be anyone who brings lived experience into focus: a teacher navigating a new curriculum, a nurse working through a staffing shortage, a small business owner dealing with inflation, or a community leader responding to a local crisis. What matters is not their uniqueness, but their proximity to stakes.

> When characters are chosen thoughtfully, they help readers understand what the issue feels like, not just what it is.

Understanding Stakes: What Changes for a Person?

Stakes answer the question: *What might this person gain or lose?* This is the emotional core of a story. Stakes can be dramatic, loss of livelihood, eviction, medical risk, but they can also be subtle. A shift in identity. A change in routine. A threat to dignity. A conflict of values. A moment of decision that forces someone to reconsider what they believe.

When journalists clarify stakes, stories gain purpose. Without stakes, even the most important issue feels distant. With stakes, even a small issue becomes compelling.

This is why Maria's snowplow story in Section 1.1 transformed only after she met residents. What was once a policy vote become a story of safety, mobility, and survival because she introduced people whose lives were shaped by that decision.

Conflict: The Force That Moves Story Forward

Conflict is often misunderstood as chaos, argument, or drama. But in journalism, conflict is simply **tension**. It emerges whenever there is change, contrast, uncertainty, or struggle. Conflict can exist between two people, but it can also exist between a community and an institution, between a person and a system, or between a community's past and future.

Examples of conflict include:

- A teacher balancing new mandates with limited resources.
- A neighborhood resisting redevelopment plans.
- A family navigating healthcare decision.
- A mayor responding to competing community demands.
- A teenager confronting misinformation online.

The power of conflict lies in what it reveals. It exposes inequities, highlights pressure points, shows what matters most, and uncovers deeper systemic issues that might otherwise go unnoticed.

> Journalists should treat conflict with responsibility. Conflict should clarify, not sensationalize. It should reveal the truth, not distort it. When handled carefully, conflict becomes the engine that moves a story forward while keeping its moral center intact.

Choosing the Right Characters and Conflicts

A story becomes stronger when the journalist selects characters who represent the stakes truthfully. This requires sensitivity and discernment. Reporters must avoid choosing characters simply because they are emotional, outspoken, or convenient. They must avoid relying on stereotypes or token figures who reinforce clichés about race, class, or region. This is especially important in place-based storytelling where certain communities, like Appalachia, inner-city neighborhoods, or immigrant enclaves, have long histories of being portrayed inaccurately.

Instead, journalists must seek characters who offer nuanced perspectives. They should ask:

- Does this person reflect the broader issue without being reduced to a symbol?
- Does their experience illuminate the stakes honestly?
- Do they add complexity to the story?
- Are we hearing from people who are often overlooked or overshadowed?

These questions help ensure that character-driven storytelling remains responsible and representative.

Depth Over Drama

A common mistake beginners make is choosing characters solely for dramatic effect. But journalism is not entertainment. A woman crying in front of a burned building does not automatically make her the best character for a fire story. A loud protester does not represent an entire movement. A controversial quote does not define a community's identity.

Good characters are not sensational, they are relevant. Their presence deepens understanding rather than distracting from it.

Depth matters more than drama.

How Characters, Conflict and Stakes Shape Story Structure

Once characters and stakes are clear, structure becomes easier. Stories often take shape through the path of the character's experience:

- What do they want?
- What prevents them from getting it?
- What pressures shape their decisions?
- What changes, for better or worse?

> This is the foundation of narrative arc, even in non-fiction reporting. Strong characters create clarity. Clear stakes create urgency. Identifiable conflict creates direction.

This does not mean the story must follow one person; multiple characters can offer multiple perspectives. But the journalist must choose wisely and avoid overloading the narrative with too many competing voices. Too many characters fragment focus; too few oversimplify reality. Finding the balance is part of responsible storytelling.

When Character Choice Becomes Ethical

Selecting characters can also raise ethical considerations. A person who is vulnerable, traumatized, or marginalized may have deeply compelling stakes, but that does not mean their pain should be placed on public display. Journalists must consider whether including them serves the public interest or merely satisfies curiosity.

For example, interviewing a grieving mother may reveal important truths, but doing so without sensitivity can cause harm. Focusing excessively on one troubled teenager may reinforce negative stereotypes about an entire neighborhood. Choosing a single outspoken resident may misrepresent a community's diversity of opinions.

Ethical character selection requires more than access, it requires care.

Case Illustration: How Character Choice Changes a Story

Imagine a journalist covering a dispute over a new zoning proposal. If the reporter interviews only officials, the story becomes bureaucratic. If the reporter interviews only angry activists, the story becomes one-dimensional conflict. But if the journalist finds a family whose home sits at the center of the development plan, people who have lived in the neighborhood for decades, the stakes become visible. Their experience connects policy to lived reality.

Choosing the right characters transforms a procedural issue into a story about belonging, displacement, identity, and community change. The zoning issue remains the same; the meaning becomes clearer and deeper.

Integrating Characters & Conflict into Story Judgment

By this point in the chapter, students should see that story strength depends not only on ideas or events, but on the lived experiences that animate them. Characters reveal the human dimension behind news values. Conflict highlights the forces shaping those lives. Stakes clarify why the story matters.

This is why characters are central to story selection, not just story writing. Before a reporter writes the first sentence, they must already understand who is affected, why it matters, and where the story's tension lives.

Strong journalism begins before the draft. It begins with people.

JOURNALISM'S ROLE IN STORYTELLING

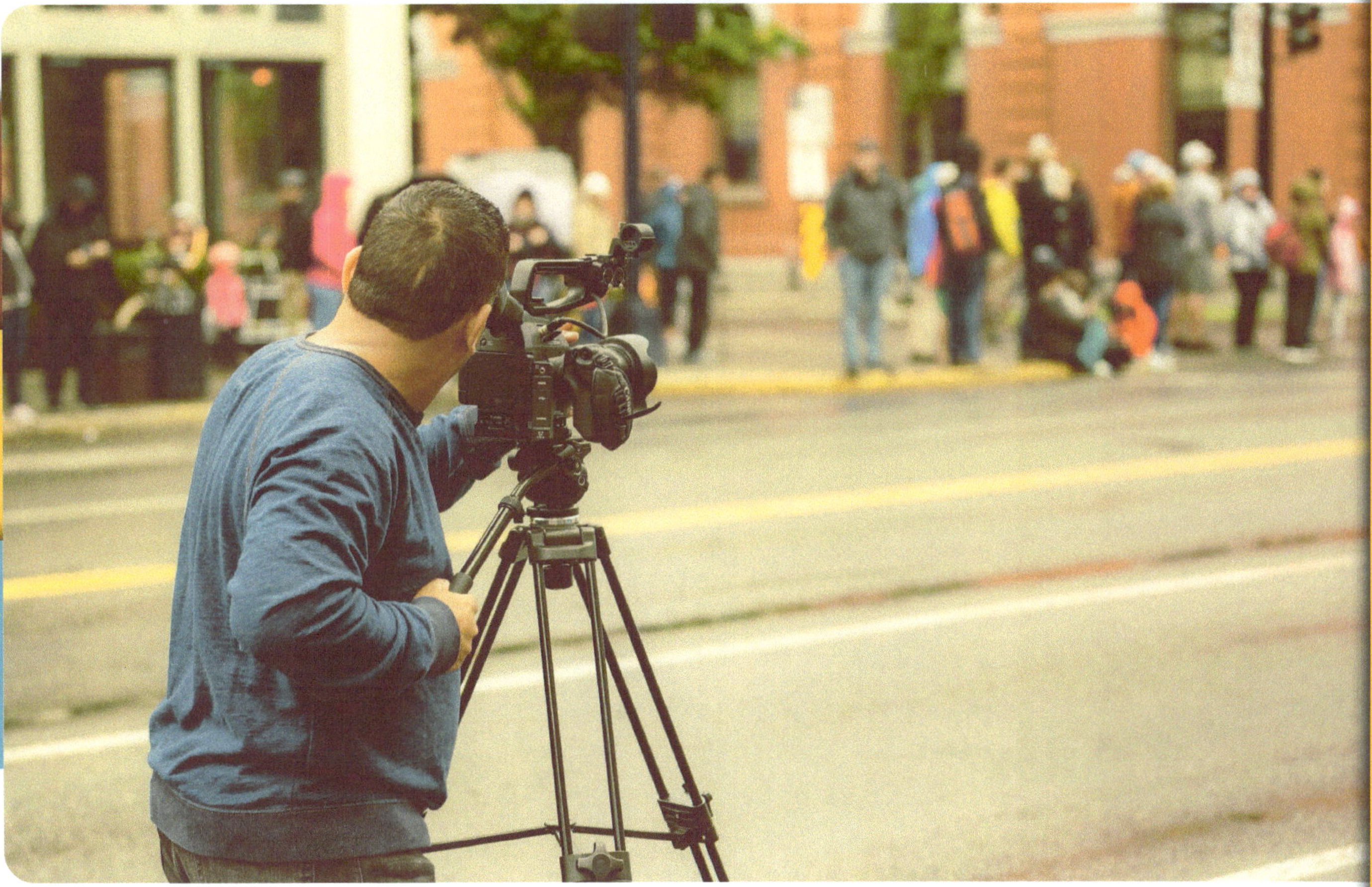

PLACED-BASED LEARNING SERIES

Overview

Journalism is more than the act of writing. At its core, journalism is a public service that informs communities, exposes truths, builds civic understanding, and strengthens democratic participation. This chapter explores the essential role journalism plays in society, how it differs from other forms of communication, and why ethics, verification, and transparency are foundational to its practice. Through real-world examples, ethical frameworks, practical tools, and a detailed case study, students will learn how journalism transforms storytelling into public accountability.

Section 2.1 : Journalism as Public Service

Journalism has always existed at the intersection of storytelling and public responsibility. It is not simply the act of writing, nor is it a creative outlet built on personal voice alone. Journalism is rooted in a civic mission that demands accuracy, accountability, and a deliberate process of verification. To understand journalism's role in storytelling, students must first understand how journalism distinguishes itself from blogging, commentary, platform content, and the many persuasive forms of communication competing for public attention today.

Anecdote: The Story That Missed Its Purpose

Early in her reporting experience, Hannah believed she had uncovered an important story about the ongoing campus housing shortage. Her draft was lively and impassioned, filled with quotes from frustrated students and pointed criticism of the administration. But what she had not done was confirm the central claim that "the university had ignored students' needs for years." The sentence emerged more from her personal interpretation than from evidence. When her professor asked where she found that claim, the entire story unraveled. Though Hannah's intentions were good, she had produced commentary, not journalism. That moment helped her understand journalism's true purpose: not to echo personal impressions but to supply the public with verified, contextual information it can use.

Her experience illustrates a foundational truth. A story may sound urgent and convincing, but if it is not anchored in a disciplined reporting process, one built on verification, context, independence, and ethical responsibility, it cannot serve the public. Journalism demands more than expression; it demands service.

Journalism as a Civic Institution

At the heart of journalism is an obligation to the public. This obligation is not optional and does not depend on a reporter's experience level, medium, or audience size. Whether covering a city council meeting or a national investigation, a journalist's work contributes to the civic life of a community. Journalism exists to strengthen democratic decision-making, hold institutions accountable, illuminate problems and solutions, and give audiences a fair understanding of events unfolding around them.

This mission is what separates journalism from other forms of storytelling. Blogs may inform or entertain, commentary may persuade, and influencer content may inspire, but journalism operates under a disciplined method. Its purpose is not expression or persuasion; it is public understanding. This distinction becomes even more critical in a media environment saturated with personal opinions masquerading as facts and with platforms that reward speed and outrage more than accuracy.

What Makes Journalism Unique?

To fully grasp journalism's place in storytelling, students need to understand the four characteristics that give journalism its identity. The first is verification. Verification is not a single action but an ongoing process. Journalists do not publish an interview because a source "seems trustworthy." They corroborate details through additional interviews, review documents, compare accounts, and challenge inconsistencies. The goal is not to support a particular narrative but to discover what is factual and what remains uncertain.

Second is context. A fact without context can mislead more than it informs. If a crime rate goes up, how significant is the increase? Is it a one-year anomaly or part of a trend? What factors might explain it? Who is affected? Journalists provide readers with the information needed to interpret facts correctly. Without context, audiences are left vulnerable to simplistic or sensational interpretations, which can distort understanding.

Third, journalism requires independence. Independence protects the integrity of reporting. Journalists cannot allow their coverage to be shaped by political allegiances, financial incentives, personal relationships, or institutional pressures. Independence ensures that the pursuit of truth is free from hidden motives.

Finally, journalism is defined by its commitment to public service. It prioritizes what audiences need to know, not what will generate the most clicks or affirm personal beliefs. This sense of responsibility is what keeps journalism grounded even when reporting on emotionally charged or politically sensitive topics.

Journalism vs. Blogging, Commentary, and Platform Content

Students often assume journalism is simply "writing something factual," but the differences become clear when comparing journalism to neighboring genres. A blog may include information, but bloggers are not required to verify details or present contrasting viewpoints. Commentary and opinion writing are valid forms of communication but are driven by argumentation rather than verification. Influencer content, social-media threads, and video commentary may appear journalistic at times, but they rarely demonstrate the transparency, independence, or ethical rigor required of professional reporting.

A blog may include information, but bloggers are not required to verify details or present contrasting viewpoints.

> Journalism, by contrast, demands a transparent, evidence-based approach. It shows audiences how information was gathered, acknowledges what is unknown, and avoids presenting personal opinion as fact. Journalism uses storytelling techniques, but storytelling alone does not make journalism. The method is what matters.

Real-World Examples: Journalism Done Well and Journalism Gone Wrong

A helpful way to understand journalism's responsibilities is to examine how verification and ethics influence outcomes in real reporting. The Washington Post's investigation known as *The Afghanistan Papers* illustrates responsible journalism in action. Reporters obtained thousands of pages of government interviews and documentation, verified them through independent sources, and presented the material with transparency. The investigation held powerful institutions accountable and provided clarity on a matter of national importance. It demonstrated how thorough verification and independence enable journalism to serve the public good.

A helpful way to understand journalism's responsibilities is to examine how verification and ethics influence outcomes in real reporting.

Contrast this with reporting failures during the 2014 Ebola outbreak, when some Western outlets published misleading portrayals of West African communities. These stories framed entire regions as chaotic or uninformed, ignoring the structured and intelligent local responses already in place. The issue was not only factual accuracy; it was a lack of nuance, cultural understanding, and contextual reporting. Stereotypes filled the gaps where verification should have been.

A similar pattern appears in harmful coverage of Appalachia. Reporters who visit briefly, often during crises, tend to rely on pre-existing narratives of poverty, addiction, or cultural backwardness. These stories flatten diverse communities into caricatures because reporters skip the critical steps of listening, contextualizing, and verifying. Journalism becomes distorted when its method collapses.

> These examples highlight a simple truth: journalism can build understanding or deepen misunderstanding. The difference lies in process, care, and ethical discipline.

Craft Guidance: Practicing Journalism as Public Service

For students learning to report, the most important habit is to approach each story with humility and curiosity. Strong journalists begin not with answers, but with questions. They ask how they know what they think they know. They examine assumptions, both their own and those embedded in public narratives. They prioritize clarity over drama and accuracy over speed.

Transparency is essential. Audiences should understand how information was gathered, what sources were consulted, and where limitations exist. Disclosing what is uncertain does not weaken a story; it reinforces trust. The public does not expect journalists to know everything, but it does expect them to be honest about what they know and how they know it.

Equally important is the journalist's responsibility to represent communities accurately. Reporting must go beyond official voices and include individuals directly affected by an issue. Journalists cannot rely on a single viewpoint, nor can they treat one anecdote as representative of an entire community. Public-service journalism requires broad listening and fair presentation.

Cross-Cultural and Ethical Considerations

Stories that involve cultural difference, trauma, or historically marginalized communities require additional care. Context is crucial, as misunderstandings can easily reinforce harmful stereotypes. Some communities distrust institutions for reasons rooted in history; others may interpret certain questions or behaviors differently because of cultural norms. Journalists must remain aware that their presence carries power, and they must navigate that power with respect.

> Ethical journalism begins with empathy. It requires the reporter to consider who may be harmed, even unintentionally, by the way a story is framed. Accuracy is not purely factual, it includes cultural accuracy, contextual accuracy, and emotional accuracy. These principles ensure that journalism informs rather than harms.

Common Mistakes and How to Avoid Them

New reporters often make predictable errors. They may confuse passion with evidence or publish details before verifying them. Some rely heavily on official sources without seeking community perspectives. Others unintentionally adopt stereotypes or fill information gaps with assumptions. These pitfalls can be avoided through consistent adherence to process: verify facts, seek diverse voices, question assumptions, and be transparent about limitations.

Reflection Activity

To better understand journalism's role as public service, students should identify a current local issue and examine how reporting on that issue could meaningfully help the community. Consider what verification would be required, which voices should be included, and how the story might look different if approached from a perspective of service rather than expression. Write a one-page reflection explaining how journalistic decisions, including sourcing, context, language, and transparency, shape public understanding of the issue.

Section 2.2: Ethics, Verification, and Transparency

Journalism is built on a series of ethical commitments that give the profession its credibility. These commitments are not theoretical ideals reserved for major investigations; they are daily practices that shape how journalists gather information, interact with sources, verify facts, present narratives, and correct mistakes. Ethics, verification, and transparency form the backbone of public trust, and without them, even the most compelling story loses its value.

Ethics, verification, and transparency form the backbone of public trust, and without them, even the most compelling story loses its value.

Anecdote: The Error That Couldn't Be Ignored

When Talia wrote her first major profile for the student newspaper, she felt confident. She had spent an hour interviewing a local community organizer, taken several pages of notes, and crafted a narrative that captured the emotional urgency of the organizer's work. The article went live the next morning, and for a few hours, everything seemed perfect.

That changed when her phone buzzed with a message from the organizer: *"I never said that."*

Talia reread her notes and realized the problem immediately. The quote she published wasn't verbatim; it was her interpretation of what the organizer meant, reshaped into direct speech. What felt like a small creative choice became a serious ethical breach the moment it reached the public.

Her editor sat her down and explained that misquoting, even unintentionally, can damage credibility, harm relationships with sources, and mislead readers. It can retraumatize a subject, undermine a community's trust in the newsroom, or distort the public record. Talia understood that accuracy is not a detail, it is the foundation of ethical journalism.

Understanding Why Ethics Matter

Ethics in journalism exist to ensure fairness, accuracy, and respect for the people whose lives are affected by reporting. Unlike commentary or marketing, journalism carries a responsibility to truth and public service. Ethical considerations shape every stage of reporting, from the first interview question to the final sentence published.

The SPJ Code of Ethics, widely recognized across the profession — provides a framework that encapsulates the values journalists rely on when navigating complex decisions. Although simple in appearance, its principles require thoughtful interpretation and daily discipline. The code rests on four pillars: **Seek truth and report it. Minimize harm. Act independently. Be accountable.**

Each principle supports the others. Truth without fairness can harm. Independence without accountability can lead to bias. Transparency without verification is meaningless. Ethical journalism requires the balance of all four.

Verification: The Core of Responsible Reporting

Verification is the process that separates journalism from rumor, commentary, or personal belief. It is a deliberate effort to confirm information, challenge assumptions, and ensure accuracy. Verification is rarely glamorous. It involves slow, meticulous tasks like cross-checking names, confirming timelines, reviewing documents, and contacting additional sources.

Students often imagine verification as something required only in long investigations, but it is just as essential in daily stories. A misreported date or misidentified individual can cause real harm. Journalists verify because the public relies on accuracy to make informed decisions.

A misreported date or misidentified individual can cause real harm.

To guide beginning reporters, it can be helpful to think of verification as a series of habits:

- **Identify every factual claim** that needs confirmation.
- **Seek out multiple perspectives**, especially on contentious issues.
- **Cross-check quotes with recordings or written notes.**
- **Clarify contradictions** rather than accepting one side's account.
- **Review documents and data** that support or challenge claims.
- **Acknowledge what is unknown**, instead of filling gaps with assumptions.

These habits prevent errors like Talia's, small mistakes that grow large once published.

Transparency: Showing the Reader How You Know

Trust increases when audiences understand the process behind reporting. Transparency is not about overloading the reader with detail, but about being clear enough that the reader can judge the fairness and reliability of the work.

> Journalists practice transparency when they explain how interviews were conducted, disclose what information could not be obtained, describe why certain sources declined to speak, or clarify the limits of available data. These disclosures signal honesty.

For example, writing "State officials declined to provide data on maternal care outcomes" gives readers insight into the obstacles faced during reporting and shows that the journalist pursued answers beyond what appears in the final story. Transparency also includes correcting mistakes promptly and publicly, not quietly adjusting a digital article without acknowledgement.

Independence: Protecting the Integrity of Reporting

Independence ensures that journalism serves the public rather than powerful interests. It requires journalists to avoid conflicts of interest, financial influence, or personal relationships that could distort coverage. Independence also means resisting pressure from political groups, advertisers, or even friendly sources hoping to influence the narrative.

For students, independence often begins with a simple question: *"Who might benefit from this story being told this way?"* That question encourages critical thinking about motives, both internal and external. It guides reporters to avoid becoming advocates for a particular side, even when they empathize deeply with individuals involved in the story.

Independence is not emotional detachment; it is fairness. A journalist can empathize with sources while still maintaining boundaries that protect the integrity of the reporting.

Accountability: Lessons in Owning Mistakes

Journalists inevitably make mistakes. The ethical response is not to hide them but to correct them visibly and reflectively. Accountability reinforces trust by showing that journalism is a process, one committed to truth, not ego.

A newsroom that corrects errors sends a message: accuracy matters more than pride. For students, practicing accountability might involve acknowledging where their reporting fell short, clarifying misinterpretations, or explaining methodological constraints. These steps demonstrate respect for the audience and for the subjects of the story.

Accountability reinforces trust by showing that journalism is a process, one committed to truth, not ego.

When Ethics Break Down: Lessons from Real-world Failures

Ethical failures in journalism often stem from the same root problems: rushing to publish, failing to verify claims, misrepresenting communities, or leaning on stereotypes. Reporting during crises, for instance, often results in misidentification or unverified rumours that spread faster than corrections.

Coverage of the 2014 Ebola outbreak offers a clear case of ethical failure. Several Western outlets portrayed West African communities as chaotic or uninformed, ignoring the organized, culturally grounded responses local health workers developed. The problem was not only factual inaccuracy, but also a profound lack of context, a failure to ask deeper questions and listen to local voices. This kind of framing can cause long-term harm by reinforcing racialized and cultural misconceptions.

Similarly, parachute journalism in Appalachia often results in stories that flatten complex communities into stereotypes. When journalists fail to verify through diverse sources or look beyond the most dramatic anecdotes, they tell stories that misrepresent rather than illuminate. This erodes community trust and contradicts the journalist's ethical obligation to minimize harm.

These examples serve as reminders that ethical journalism requires humility, patience, and a willingness to listen.

Developing an Ethical Practice

Students can cultivate strong ethical instincts by building routines rather than relying on after-the-fact corrections. Good routines include checking assumptions, questioning the origin of information, consulting a diverse range of voices, and considering the broader consequences of reporting choices. Ethical practice also means embedding respect into reporting, treating sources as people, not soundbites, and ensuring stories reflect lived realities rather than convenient narratives.

Verification and ethics flourish when journalists understand the stakes of their work. Every story has the potential to inform, mislead, empower, or harm. Every choice, which voices to include, which facts to highlight, which words to use, contributes to the story's impact.

Ethical practice also means embedding respect into reporting, treating sources as people, not soundbites, and ensuring stories reflect lived realities rather than convenient narratives.

Reflection Activity

Choose a recent news story from a reputable national outlet and identify one moment where verification, transparency, or ethical consideration made the reporting stronger. Then, identify one moment where more context or additional verification might have improved clarity or minimized harm. Write a short reflection explaining how these elements shape the reader's understanding.

Section 2.3: Case Study: *Lost Mothers* (ProPublica & NPR)

Investigative journalism often reveals its power most clearly when it breaks open a problem the public never realized existed. *Lost Mothers*, the landmark investigation by ProPublica and NPR, did precisely that. Before the series, maternal mortality in the United States was treated as a statistical problem, often minimized or misunderstood, and poorly tracked by federal agencies. By the time the work was completed, it had reshaped national awareness, prompted policy changes, and established a new standard for public-service reporting.

Unlike daily news stories, this project required an extraordinary blend of verification, ethics, trauma-sensitive interviewing, and transparency. It also demanded an understanding of systems, medical, political, social, and institutional, that shaped maternal outcomes. This section examines the *Lost Mothers* investigation not simply as a story, but as a model of how journalism serves the public interest with rigor and humanity.

The Problem: A Crisis Hidden in Plain Sight

The United States has the highest maternal mortality rate among developed nations, yet for years this crisis remained fragmented and underreported. Many states had unreliable or outdated reporting systems. Deaths were misclassified, undercounted, or categorized in ways that concealed underlying causes. Hospitals were inconsistent in how they documented complications. Families grieving the loss of a mother often received vague explanations, or none at all.

The public impression was that maternal deaths were extremely rare, the result of unavoidable medical complications. The ProPublica and NPR team discovered that many deaths were preventable, that systemic gaps contributed to delayed interventions, and that the nation lacked a consistent way to track these tragedies.

This gap in public understanding shaped how the journalists approached the story. The project's purpose was not only to reveal individual cases but to expose a pattern invisible to policymakers and the public alike.

A Human Entry Point

The series opens with the story of a young mother who died shortly after childbirth — a narrative offered with restraint, clarity, and deep respect. The writing does not sensationalize her final moments or exploit grief for effect. Instead, it invites the reader to see the world as her family experienced it: joy, confusion, fear, then shock and unanswered questions.

Beginning with a human story isn't a dramatic technique but an ethical and narrative choice. It sets an emotional anchor that guides the reader into the broader systemic issues, reminding them that behind every statistic is a real life interrupted. In doing so, the story maintains dignity, emphasizing the family's agency and experience rather than using them as symbols.

Building the Evidence: A Database That Didn't Exist

One of the most ambitious elements of the investigation was the team's decision to create their own national database of maternal deaths, a task that federal institutions had not undertaken thoroughly. This process involved hundreds of hours of verification. The journalists examined obituaries, filed public record requests, contacted state agencies, reviewed death certificates, and interviewed families. They worked with medical experts to interpret hospital records and identify gaps in documentation.

Their database eventually included thousands of complications and hundreds of confirmed maternal deaths. The creation of this database demonstrates a fundamental principle of public-service journalism: when institutions fail to track a critical issue, reporters can fill the void through disciplined, transparent work.

Although the investigative process is rigorous, the writing remains accessible. Readers are not overwhelmed with numbers; instead, the analysis supports the narrative, revealing patterns that would otherwise remain hidden.

Explaining the System: Why Mothers Were Dying

The investigation uncovered recurring failures across hospitals and healthcare systems:

- Delays in recognizing warning signs
- Inconsistent emergency protocols
- Poor communication between providers
- Lack of postpartum follow-up
- Racial disparities in how symptoms were treated
- Gaps in training and staffing

These problems were not isolated incidents. They formed a pattern that pointed to systemic breakdown. The reporting connects these failures not to individual blame but to structural issues: fragmented healthcare oversight, lack of standardized practices, and inadequate national data.

The explanatory sections of the series demonstrate how journalism can translate complex medical and policy failures into language the public can understand. This is where narrative and reporting intersect: the story is compelling not because it is emotional, but because it is explained with clarity and grounded in verified evidence.

Ethics in Trauma Reporting

A significant part of the project involves interviewing families who had experienced devastating loss. The journalists approached each conversation with sensitivity, ensuring that participation was voluntary and that families understood how their stories would be used. They allowed relatives to explain events in their own words, often revisiting timelines together to ensure factual accuracy.

Importantly, the writing avoids unnecessary detail. There are no graphic depictions, no exaggerated language, no dramatization. The focus remains on the family's experience and the systems that failed them. The team's ethical approach reinforces an important lesson for student journalists: reporting on trauma requires care, patience, and respect.

The journalists also balanced the emotional narratives with institutional responses. Hospitals, medical boards, and state agencies were contacted for comment. When an institution declined to speak, the reporting was transparent about that refusal. This approach allows readers to see both the human impact and the systemic context.

Holding Power Accountable

A critical component of accountability journalism is confronting those responsible, not aggressively, but clearly and factually. The *Lost Mothers* team did this by:

- presenting verified cases to hospital systems
- questioning state agencies about flawed reporting processes
- comparing U.S. maternal outcomes with international data
- documenting where protocols failed
- highlighting where institutions refused to answer questions

When hospitals disagreed with the findings, their statements were included fairly. When they declined comment, that silence became part of the story. Accountability is not about accusation; it is about transparency. The investigation gave the public information that institutions were unwilling or unable to provide.

Impact: How the Reporting Changed Policy

One of the most remarkable outcomes of *Lost Mothers* is the measurable impact it had on public policy. The investigation prompted states to create or strengthen maternal mortality review committees, adopt standard protocols for postpartum care, and improve data collection. Congressional hearings were held. Hospitals revised training and emergency procedures.

Journalism rarely solves a problem alone, but it can expose the truth in ways that empower policymakers, medical institutions, and communities to act. This case demonstrates journalism's role not just as storyteller, but as a force that brings critical issues out of the shadows and into public consciousness.

Journalism rarely solves a problem alone, but it can expose the truth in ways that empower policymakers, medical institutions, and communities to act.

Borrowing From the Case: What Students Can Learn

For emerging journalists, *Lost Mothers* offers several practical lessons that reflect the principles introduced earlier in this chapter:

- **Begin with real human experience**, not to dramatize but to humanize.
- **Use systems thinking** to move from individual stories to broader patterns.
- **Verify relentlessly**, especially when institutions fail to provide reliable data.
- **Explain complex information clearly**, without oversimplifying.
- **Treat vulnerable sources with dignity and patience.**

- **Be transparent about limits**, including incomplete data or institutional silence.
- **Invite accountability** by soliciting responses from those in power.

These lessons are not theoretical; they are demonstrated throughout every stage of the project.

Discussion Questions

1. How does *Lost Mothers* balance emotional storytelling with rigorous reporting?
2. What verification steps were most critical to ensuring the accuracy of the investigation?
3. How did the journalists' ethical approach shape the way the story was told?
4. In what ways does systems thinking strengthen public-service reporting?
5. How might a similar investigation be conducted at the student or local level?

Key Takeaways

The *Lost Mothers* investigation stands as a powerful example of journalism fulfilling its public-service mission. It combines clear storytelling with exhaustive verification, ethical sensitivity with accountability, and human experience with systemic insight. Its success lies not in dramatic language but in the disciplined, respectful approach the journalists took with every detail. For students, it serves as a model of how journalism can reveal truths that institutions overlook, and how those truths can drive meaningful change.

BJP hit back
Packed fruits and vegetables
Solar water heaters
KBK Infographics

CHAPTER 3

CHARACTERS, CONFLICT & RESOLUTION IN REPORTING

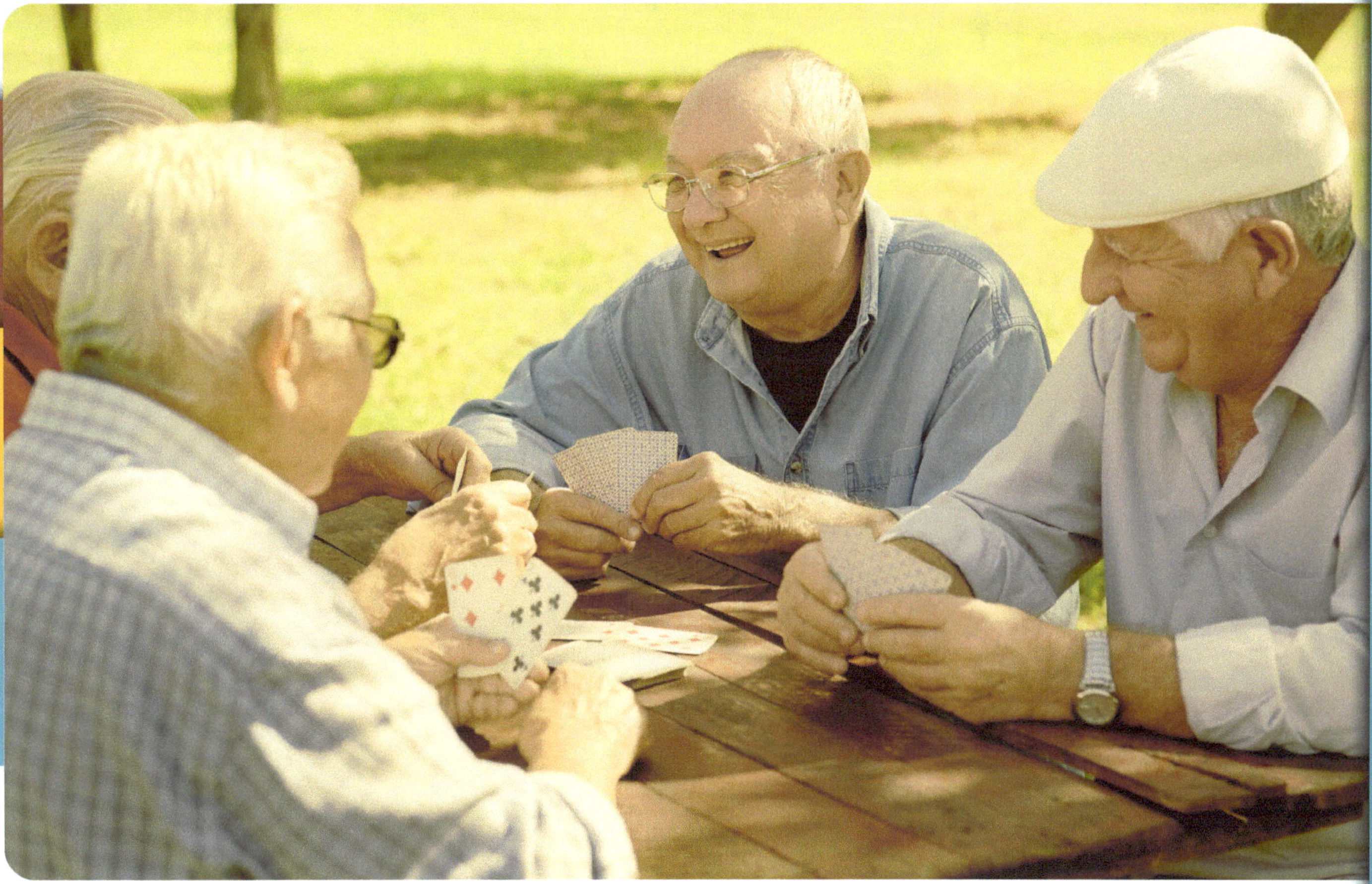

PLACED-BASED LEARNING SERIES

Overview

Journalism depends on people. Whether the story explores a policy change, a community challenge, or a systemic issue shaped over decades, characters give the narrative emotional grounding and help audiences understand why the story matters. Every reported story, no matter how data-heavy or institution-focused—has human consequences. In this chapter, students will learn how to identify the right characters for a story, how to represent them ethically, and how to avoid the stereotypes that emerge when reporters focus on convenience instead of context.

The chapter also explores what "conflict" means in journalism. Conflict is not merely argument, disagreement, or drama. Journalistic conflict emerges from pressure points: competing interests, systemic failures, policy impacts, inequities, or unresolved questions that shape real lives. Students will learn to identify the deeper layers of conflict, structural, historical, institutional, and to portray these tensions without exaggeration or bias.

Finally, this chapter examines the journalistic idea of "resolution." Unlike fiction, journalism rarely offers perfect closure. Instead, resolution means giving the audience a clear understanding of the movement within a situation: what is changing, where tensions remain, and what questions still need answers. A strong journalistic resolution tells the truth about complexity while providing readers with the tools to understand it.

By examining real-world examples, case studies, and practical reporting strategies, students will learn to choose strong and representative characters, explain conflict responsibly, and write stories that illuminate systems rather than reinforce stereotypes. Throughout the chapter, students will also encounter activities, common pitfalls, and checklists that strengthen their ability to craft character-driven, conflict-aware reporting rooted in public service.

Section 3.1: Understanding Characters in Journalism

Journalism begins with people. Even the most complex topics, healthcare policy, environmental regulation, economic shifts, education reform, ultimately affect human beings, and audiences understand these issues best through the individuals who experience them. Characters in journalism are not fictional constructions; they are real people whose experiences give life and meaning to broader issues. When chosen thoughtfully and represented responsibly, they help readers see why a story matters and what's at stake.

Characters give a story its emotional gravity. They help the audience grasp abstract issues, navigate unfamiliar systems, and witness the lived consequences of decisions made by those in power. A character can transform a data-heavy topic into something human and immediate. But journalists cannot simply choose any person for this role. Strong characters must be representative, relevant, and connected to the deeper meaning of the story. If chosen carelessly, characters can distort the truth, reinforce stereotypes, or reduce a community to a single tragic or sensational narrative.

Characters in journalism are not fictional constructions; they are real people whose experiences give life and meaning to broader issues.

> This section introduces students to the purpose of characters in journalism, how to identify the right ones, and how to portray them with fairness, depth, and empathy. Characters should illuminate systems, not replace them. They should help audiences understand a story's stakes, not distract from them. Effective character-driven reporting reveals complexity, not caricature.

Anecdote: When the Wrong Character Confused the Story

During a local reporting assignment, a student journalist named Miguel was tasked with covering the closure of a public library branch. He interviewed the first person he encountered, a frustrated college student using the library as a study space. She gave an emotional account of losing her quiet spot on campus, and Miguel centered her in his story. The finished article painted the closure as a crisis for students, focusing on academic convenience and late-night study habits.

But Miguel had missed the point.

The library branch primarily served immigrants, senior citizens, and low-income families who used its language classes, after-school tutoring, computer access, and community events. By choosing a character who represented only a fraction of the library's impact, Miguel unintentionally distorted the story. His narrative was compelling, but it was incomplete and unrepresentative. His editor explained that strong journalism doesn't begin with whoever is most available or most articulate, it begins with understanding the story's true center.

Miguel realized that selecting the right character is not a matter of convenience. It is a matter of accuracy, fairness, and context.

Why Characters Matter in Journalism

Characters help readers make sense of the world. They bring concrete detail to abstract issues and serve as a bridge between individual experience and systemic reality.

> When journalism is abstract, audiences may struggle to connect emotionally or understand the stakes. When it is purely institutional, readers may feel distanced from the impact. But when real people enter the story—with nuance, context, and complexity, audiences gain a deeper understanding of how policies, systems, and events shape lives.

Characters:

- **ground the story in reality,** giving readers a focal point
- **expose the stakes,** showing what is gained or lost
- **reveal systemic forces,** helping readers see beyond the individual
- **offer emotional resonance,** making the issue feel immediate
- **provide context from lived experience,** not just official viewpoints

However, strong characters do more than evoke sympathy. They illuminate patterns. Effective journalism uses individuals to represent broader truths, not exceptions. A character is not chosen simply because they are expressive or available, but because their experience helps explain the story's deeper meaning.

A character is not chosen simply because they are expressive or available, but because their experience helps explain the story's deeper meaning.

How to Choose Strong, Representative Characters

Selecting characters is one of the most important decisions in reporting. A story's fairness, accuracy, and impact depend on who gets to speak.

1. Start by identifying the core issue.

Ask: *"What is this story truly about?"* The answer will guide you toward individuals whose lives reflect that issue.

2. Consider who is most affected.

Often the best characters are not the loudest or most accessible, but the ones who experience the consequences most directly.

3. Avoid defaulting to the "easy" interview.

People who are nearby, outspoken, or privileged are often easier to access—but may not represent the community most affected.

4. Seek diversity within the story lens.

If an issue affects multiple groups differently, more than one character may be necessary to capture that nuance.

5. Pay attention to lived expertise.

People experiencing the issue firsthand often understand its stakes better than officials or professionals.

These principles help prevent the pitfalls Miguel faced in his library story. Journalism must reflect reality, not convenience.

Showing Systems, Not Stereotypes

Journalists face a risk when relying heavily on characters: the temptation to make one person stand in for an entire community or to treat unusual circumstances as representative. This can lead to stereotypes, oversimplification, or distorted narratives.

Stereotypes emerge when:

- a single dramatic anecdote becomes the defining example
- a community is portrayed through the lens of its struggles alone
- a character is chosen because their story is emotionally extreme rather than representative
- journalists fail to include historical or structural context

Strong reporting avoids these traps by grounding characters within the systems that shape their experiences.

For example, a story on housing insecurity should not portray tenants merely as struggling individuals. It should connect their experiences to rising rental costs, zoning policies, wage stagnation, historical discrimination, and local political dynamics. Characters are entry points, not the entirety of the story.

Characters should illuminate systems, not replace them.

Real-World Examples

Positive Example: A Character Who Reveals a System

In a feature on medical debt, *The New York Times* profiled a mother working two jobs while facing mounting emergency-room bills. Rather than presenting her as a stereotype of financial hardship, the story contextualized her experience with data on rising healthcare costs, insurance gaps, and systemic inequities. Her story functioned as a lens, not a stand-in.

Harmful Example: A Character Who Misrepresents a Community

In past coverage of Appalachia, some national outlets highlighted only individuals struggling with addiction or unemployment. The resulting narratives portrayed entire towns as hopeless or dependent, ignoring the complexity and resilience of the communities. By selecting characters who reinforced sensational narratives, these stories harmed more than they informed.

Local Example: When Character Choice Changes Interpretation

A local newspaper once covered a city's new youth curfew by interviewing only police officers and a teenager who had been detained. The resulting story made youth seem like threats and the curfew like a necessity. Missing were parents, educators, youth advocates, and teens who saw the curfew as harmful. A broader character selection would have produced a more accurate, fair story.

Craft Guidance: Representing Characters Ethically

Portraying characters in journalism requires discipline and empathy. Stories should not flatten people into symbols or plot devices.

Strong character reporting includes:

- **deep listening**, allowing people to describe their experiences in their own words
- **accurate quoting**, avoiding paraphrased exaggerations
- **attention to detail**, capturing voice, environment, and context without embellishment
- **transparency**, clarifying when information is confirmed versus described from memory
- **contextual fairness**, ensuring a character's story is presented within the broader issue

> Ethical character reporting reflects respect, respect for accuracy, respect for nuance, and respect for the people whose lives appear on the page.

Light Checklist: Choosing Characters Responsibly

- Does this person reflect the *central issue* of the story?
- Are they directly affected by the issue or only marginally connected?
- Does their experience illuminate a broader system?
- Am I avoiding stereotypes or overgeneralization?
- Have I considered multiple perspectives?

Common Pitfall: The "Stand-In" Trap

One of the most common mistakes in journalism is letting a character become a symbol of a community they do not represent. A single mother in a low-income neighborhood is not a stand-in for all single mothers. A struggling student is not a stand-in for all teenagers. A grieving father is not the voice of a whole movement.

> Characters are powerful, but they must be contextualized. They show the audience something real, but they do not speak for everyone. Good journalists resist the temptation to let convenience or emotion override nuance.

Reflection Activity

Think of an issue affecting your campus or community. Identify three potential characters you could interview. For each character, write a brief note explaining what they reveal about the issue and what limitations might arise if you centered your story solely on their perspective. Reflect on how you would balance character voice with systemic context.

Section 3.2: Identifying and Explaining Conflict

Conflict is the engine of every journalistic story. It is what creates movement, reveals stakes, and helps audiences understand why an issue matters. But conflict in journalism is frequently misunderstood. Students often default to imagining conflict as confrontation: two people arguing, institutions clashing, or opposing sides fighting for dominance. In reality, journalistic conflict is almost never about dramatizing disagreement. Instead, it is about identifying the *pressure points* that shape an issue: the tensions between what people need and what systems provide, between what is promised and what is delivered, between how things work and how they should work.

> Conflict is the presence of unresolved questions. It is the friction created when real lives collide with structural forces. And when journalists understand how conflict functions, they can write stories that illuminate not only events but the deeper forces shaping them.

Anecdote: The Story with No Real Conflict

When Nadia covered a new city recycling program, she wrote what she believed to be a strong piece: clear explanations, detailed descriptions, and quotes from two city officials announcing the project. The article included supportive comments from residents who were excited about the initiative. Her editor flagged one problem: the story had no conflict. It presented a program without exploring the challenges, gaps, or consequences. It failed to ask who benefits, who struggles, or what pressures shaped the policy.

After revisiting the issue, Nadia discovered that the new policy required residents to purchase specific containers many low-income families couldn't afford. Others worried about increased fines for non-compliance. By adding these perspectives and examining why the city structured the program the way it did, the story gained depth. The conflict wasn't a fight between two people; it was the tension between intention and impact.

Nadia realized that conflict in journalism lives in the space between policy and lived reality, between institutional logic and human experience.

What Conflict Really Means in Journalism

Journalistic conflict is not an argument. It is not a drama. It is the presence of competing needs, pressures, expectations, or consequences that affect people's lives.

To understand conflict, journalists must ask questions like:

- What problem is this story responding to?
- What factors or systems are shaping the situation?
- What expectations or promises are being challenged?
- Who is affected, and how?
- Where is the tension or unresolved issue?

In journalism, conflict often emerges from mismatches:

- between public promises and public experiences
- between policy and implementation
- between institutions and individuals
- between resources and needs
- between values and outcomes

This broader view helps students move beyond the idea that conflict is just a disagreement between two sides. Instead, conflict becomes a lens for understanding systems.

Conflict as a System, Not a Fight

Reporters sometimes default to the familiar "two sides" framing because it feels balanced or symmetrical. But many issues do not have two sides. Some have five. Some have twelve. Some have none at all, because the conflict lies not between groups but within a broken system.

Reporters sometimes default to the familiar "two sides" framing because it feels balanced or symmetrical.

Consider a story about school bus delays. It may appear at first to be a dispute between parents and school administrators. But a deeper exploration might reveal:

- driver shortages
- state funding cuts
- rising transportation costs
- competing contractor bids
- lack of transit infrastructure
- shifting district boundaries

The real conflict is not interpersonal; it is structural.

When journalists identify the true nature of conflict, they help audiences understand not only what is happening but *why*.

Avoiding Drama and Oversimplification

The danger of misrepresenting conflict is that it can distort reality. If a journalist reduces a complex issue to a simple clash, they risk exaggerating tension or manufacturing polarization that does not exist. This is especially harmful in stories involving marginalized or misunderstood communities, where oversimplified conflict can reinforce stereotypes.

> A common mistake is centering vocal individuals who express extreme views. These voices may be the loudest, but not the most representative. True conflict is found not in the loudest quotes, but in the underlying systems shaping the situation.

Another pitfall is attributing conflict to personal failings rather than structural forces. For example, coverage of homelessness often focuses on individual stories without explaining the lack of affordable housing, wage stagnation, mental-health infrastructure gaps, and local zoning policies. This framing turns a systemic conflict into an individual one, misleading the audience.

Strong journalism reveals the deeper layers of conflict, not the convenient ones

Real-World Examples of Conflict Done Well (and Poorly)

Positive Example: The Flint Water Crisis (National)

In covering the Flint water crisis, reporters who did the strongest work focused on the systemic conflict between cost-cutting decisions, environmental regulations, government responsibility, and community health. They did not frame the story as residents vs. officials in a simplistic way. Instead, they showed how bureaucratic decisions created pressure points that harmed families. This framing allowed readers to see the full scope of the crisis.

Harmful Example: Coverage of Teacher Strikes (National)

Some surface-level reporting framed teacher strikes as conflicts between teachers and administrators, ignoring long-term wage stagnation, rising classroom demands, school funding shortages, and decades of policy decisions. By reducing the issue to a "fight," these stories missed the deeper systemic tensions that made the strikes necessary.

Local Example: A Noise Ordinance Dispute

A small-town newspaper once framed a debate over a new noise ordinance as a clash between loud bar owners and irritated residents. More rigorous reporting revealed conflicts between tourism-driven business interests, outdated zoning laws, and unequal enforcement in different neighborhoods. The simplistic framing obscured the structural pressures shaping the dispute.

How Journalists Identify the True Conflict

Journalists must train themselves to look beyond the first layer of a story. Strong conflict analysis comes from asking questions that peel back assumptions and reveal forces at work beneath the surface.

Helpful questions include:

- What expectations were set—and who failed to meet them?
- What systems are creating pressure?
- What resources are limited?
- Who is responsible for decisions, and who is affected by them?
- What historical factors or policies shaped the issue?
- What questions remain unresolved?
- These inquiries push reporting into more accurate, nuanced territory.

Craft Guidance: Writing Conflict Responsibly

When representing conflict, journalists should strive for clarity and fairness without exaggerating divisions. Good reporting avoids turning conflict into spectacle. Instead, it explains the stakes, the underlying causes, and the competing pressures.

Strong conflict reporting includes:

- clear explanation of the central tension
- attention to nuance and complexity
- accurate representation of affected communities
- contextual background that helps readers understand the root causes
- multiple perspectives, not merely opposing ones
- humility about what remains uncertain or unresolved

Even emotionally charged stories should avoid sensational language. Neutral, precise description allows the facts to carry weight without distortion.

Light Checklist: Identifying Real Conflict

- Does the story explain *why* the issue exists?
- Does it show competing needs or pressures?
- Does it move beyond personal disagreements?
- Does it use characters to illuminate systems?
- Does it avoid reducing complex issues to “two sides”?
- Does it reflect the lived reality of those most affected?

These questions support reporters in recognizing where conflict truly lives.

Common Pitfall: Mistaking Noise for Conflict

In journalism, the loudest voices are not always the most important. A group protesting at city hall may attract cameras, but their presence does not automatically represent the core conflict. The real issue might lie in funding formulas, legislative delays, or institutional inertia. Noise can distract from substance.

Journalists must distinguish between what is *loud* and what is *true*.

Reflection Activity

Choose a local issue currently in the news. Write a one-page analysis identifying the real conflict behind the story. Explain what pressures, systems, or competing needs are shaping the situation, and note which people or groups are most affected. Reflect on how your understanding shifts when you move beyond surface-level disagreement.

Section 3.3: Understanding Resolution in Journalism

Resolution in journalism does not function the way it does in fiction. Journalists do not create neat endings, design satisfying conclusions, or tie up every loose thread. Real life rarely offers such clarity. What journalism *can* do is provide audiences with movement: a sense of where the story stands, what has changed, what remains uncertain, and what questions still need answers. Resolution is not closure, it is understanding.

Reporters must resist the temptation to create artificial endings for the sake of narrative neatness. Instead, they should show readers where the story leads, what paths remain open, and why the issue continues to matter. In this way, journalistic resolution is more about orientation than finality. It helps audiences grasp the implications of what they have learned and understand where the story fits within a larger system.

Journalists do not create neat endings, design satisfying conclusions, or tie up every loose thread.

Anecdote: The Story That Tried Too Hard to End

In her early reporting, a student journalist named Aisha covered a community-led initiative to improve pedestrian safety at a busy intersection. After weeks of interviewing residents, attending meetings, and observing traffic patterns, she wrote a story suggesting the neighborhood's efforts had directly led the city to approve new safety measures.

It felt satisfying, but it wasn't true.

The policy was still under review. Funding had not been allocated. And none of the proposed redesigns had been approved. Her desire for a clean, hopeful ending overshadowed the actual state of the issue. Her editor reminded her: journalism does not speak in conclusions that reality cannot support.

Aisha learned that resolution in journalism lies not in inventing outcomes but in presenting accurate context, acknowledging uncertainty, and helping readers understand what will happen next, or what is still unresolved.

What Resolution Actually Means in Reporting

Resolution is an exploration of movement. It does not guarantee closure but instead offers clarity about:

- the current state of the issue
- what has changed or is changing
- what actions have been taken
- whose voices were heard or ignored
- what questions remain unanswered

Journalistic resolution helps readers feel oriented, not misled. It answers the implicit question: *"Where do things stand now?"* Even if the answer is "We don't fully know yet," that honesty is still a form of resolution.

The goal is to guide readers without pretending that a complex system can be wrapped neatly in a single narrative.

Resolution as a Tool for Understanding Systems

When journalists present resolution effectively, they help audiences see:

- how systems respond to pressure
- where policy processes are stalled or moving
- what consequences are unfolding
- what possibilities exist for future change

Resolution can appear as:

- a description of the next steps in a legal or policy process
- a reflection on how the story fits into historical context
- an explanation of ongoing investigations
- a shift in public awareness
- a change sparked by the reporting itself

Even when a story is unresolved, the journalist can still give readers clarity about the forces at work.

Avoiding False Resolution

A common mistake occurs when reporters imply that a problem is solved because someone promised action or issued a statement. Promises are not outcomes. Announcements are not solutions. Good journalism distinguishes between intention and actual change.

False resolution may happen when:

- a journalist overstates the impact of a new policy
- reporting focuses only on immediate reactions rather than long-term

patterns

- a story centers one dramatic anecdote instead of systemic follow-up
- the reporter assumes future events will unfold without verification
- institutional statements are presented as final truth

> To avoid misleading the audience, journalists must track what *has* changed, not what *might* change.

Examples of Resolution in Journalism

Positive Example: Following Through on Policy Change

A city newspaper published a series on lead contamination in older homes. The initial story identified families affected by harmful exposure. In later reporting, the newsroom followed the story's movement: city council hearings, budget debates, landlord resistance, and rapid-response inspections. The final piece did not announce that the problem was solved, it explained the action taken, the gaps remaining, and what could happen next. This is journalistic resolution: clarity, not closure.

Harmful Example: Premature Celebration

During coverage of a rural hospital closure, one outlet reported that community fundraising efforts had "saved" the hospital based on a single press release. Months later, the hospital closed anyway. The early reporting created false hope, obscured ongoing financial issues, and misled readers. The problem was not bad intention; it was premature resolution.

Feature Example: Showing Emotional Resolution Without Overclaiming

In a feature about a teen navigating the foster-care system, the journalist did not pretend the teen's situation was resolved. Instead, the article ended with the teenager's hopes, the systemic obstacles ahead, and the support structures that were beginning to form. This held emotional truth without claiming finality.

How to Write Resolution Without Forcing It

Strong journalistic resolution comes from:

- summarizing what has been uncovered
- clarifying the current status
- noting what actions have or have not occurred
- acknowledging uncertainty
- pointing readers toward what is likely to unfold next
- avoiding predictions or promises
- resisting the urge to "tie a bow" on the story

Readers appreciate honesty more than tidy conclusions.

Light Checklist: Writing Effective Resolution

- Does the ending reflect the actual state of the issue?
- Have I included clarity without oversimplifying?
- Did I avoid suggesting an outcome that hasn't happened?
- Have I acknowledged uncertainties?
- Did I connect the ending back to the story's central tension?

Common Pitfall: The "Happy Ending" Habit

Journalists sometimes want their stories to feel hopeful or complete. But an inaccurate sense of resolution can harm audiences by giving them a false understanding of reality. Strong reporting respects complexity and leaves room for unanswered questions.

As the editor told Aisha: "Journalism isn't about finishing the story. It's about telling the truth about where the story stands."

Strong reporting respects complexity and leaves room for unanswered questions.

Case Study: Resolution in Practice, A Community Water Crisis

To illustrate how resolution works, consider a local water contamination case. A journalist covering the issue might begin with the families affected, explain the chemical leak, and uncover gaps in environmental oversight. At the story's close, the reporter could summarize the immediate developments: temporary filtration systems installed, state regulators investigating, and long-term remediation still uncertain.

Notice that nothing is "solved." Instead, the resolution provides:

- clarity about current actions
- acknowledgment of ongoing risks
- transparency about unanswered questions
- orientation toward what comes next

This is how resolution supports public understanding

Reflection Activity

Choose a published news article that ends with a statement about what happens next. Examine whether the reported resolution is factual, speculative, or incomplete. Write a one-page reflection analyzing how the ending shapes the reader's understanding and whether the resolution has been handled responsibly.

CHAPTER 4

THE POWER & PERIL OF STORY

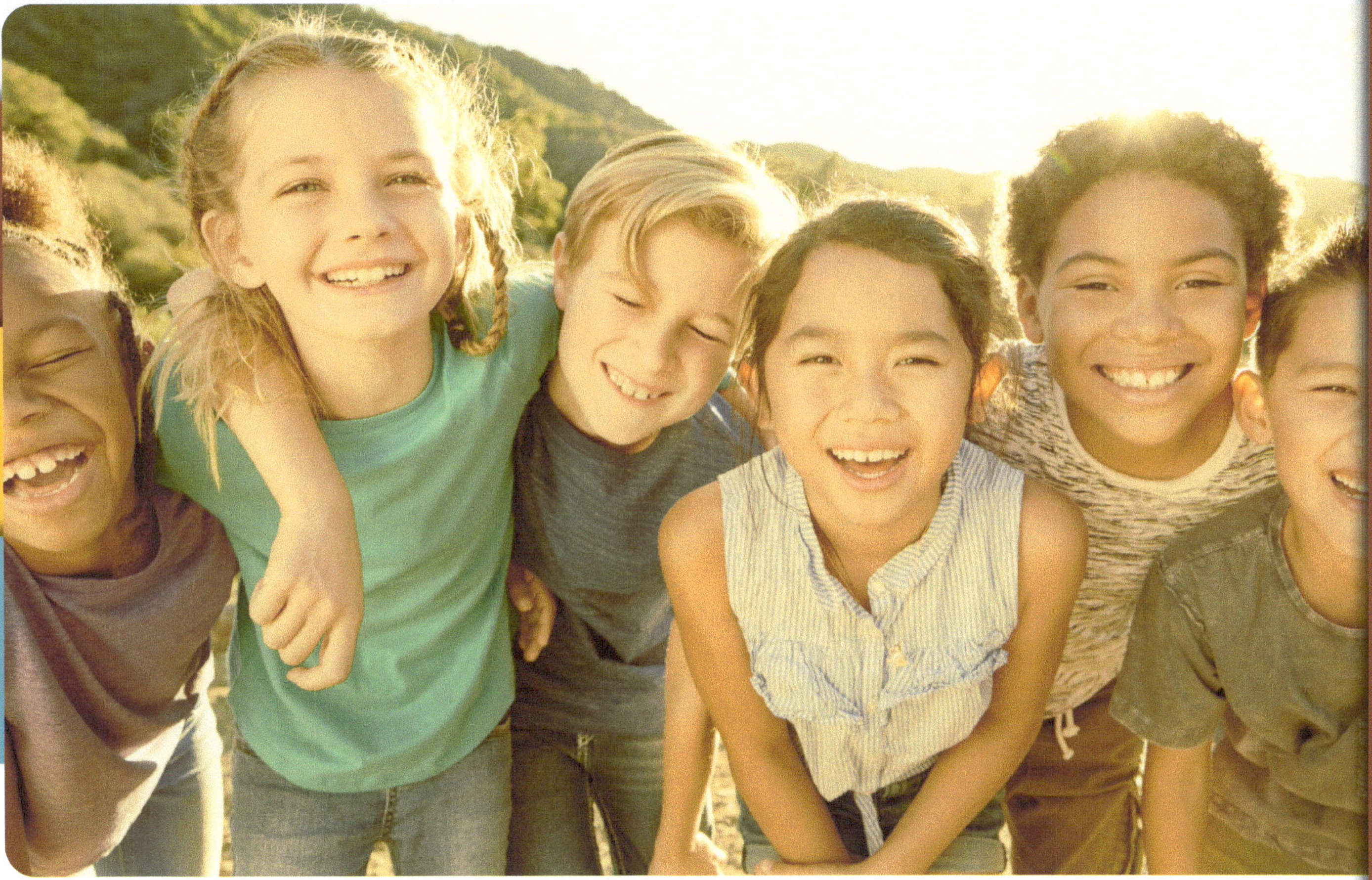

PLACED-BASED LEARNING SERIES

Overview

Stories are more than entertainment. They are frameworks through which societies interpret people, communities, and entire regions. They define who is seen as deserving of support, who is marked as a threat, and who is granted the benefit of the doubt. They influence policy decisions, institutional behavior, media framing, and the expectations people hold for themselves and others.

This chapter examines how these stories function like civic infrastructure, quietly shaping public life and structuring opportunity. Using the full Cultural Competency material you provided, we explore how certain narratives become dominant, how they produce real harm, and how communities resist and rewrite the stories imposed on them. The section concludes by establishing the foundation for understanding narrative repair and prepares for the case study that follows later in Part 3.

Understanding Harmful Narratives

Anecdote: The Story That Shaped a Community

Maria spent most of her childhood in a rural town that outsiders constantly misrepresented. To journalists, it was a place defined by failing institutions, poverty, and decline. The same reductive imagery repeated across news segments, charity campaigns, and academic reports: boarded-up buildings, isolated families, hopelessness.

But Maria's life was filled with a different reality—neighbors who shared food, elders who organized cultural gatherings, teens who volunteered at local farms, and families who supported one another through hardship. None of these truths appeared in the stories told about her home.

By the time she left for university, she noticed something unsettling: people formed opinions about her within seconds of hearing where she was from. They didn't know her community; they knew only a story that had replaced it. That story created invisible walls she had to break through every time she introduced herself.

Maria's experience reveals a critical insight: **harmful narratives can shape a community's fate more powerfully than the truth itself.**

What Harmful Narratives Are

A harmful narrative is a simplified or distorted story that reduces a group to a narrow identity. It removes complexity, erases historical context, and often frames a community through deficiency, danger, or failure. Over time, repeated narratives can harden into public assumptions. They become so normalized that people stop questioning them.

> These narratives are destructive not because they are always entirely false, but because they are incomplete. A partial truth presented as the whole truth becomes a lie by omission.

Harmful narratives do not stay on screens or pages, they shape how institutions behave, how resources are distributed, and how individuals are treated. They seep into the expectations teachers have of students, the assumptions employers hold about applicants, and the stereotypes strangers carry into interactions.

How Harmful Narratives Grow

Harmful narratives do not spread randomly; they follow a pattern that makes them durable.

They gain strength when the same message is repeated across institutions: schools, media, government, and entertainment. Once these stories are framed as objective or "common sense," they influence decisions at every level of society. Policies become written around them. Budgets respond to them. The general public internalizes them.

> This process turns a biased narrative into a structure, something people live inside without realizing it.

Examples of Narrative Harm Across Communities

Below is your Cultural Competency content rewritten in narrative form, keeping detail but minimizing bullets.

Indigenous Peoples have been framed as "disappearing," a myth that erases present-day Indigenous nations, political sovereignty, and cultural continuity. This narrative justifies treating Indigenous identity as historical rather than modern and living.

Black Americans have faced narratives focused on pathology—deficient families, criminal danger, welfare dependency. These stories ignore systemic racism and instead blame individuals for conditions created by discriminatory policies.

Asian Americans experience the "model minority" myth, which oversimplifies their experiences and hides socioeconomic diversity. The narrative also casts them as perpetual foreigners, no matter how many generations they have lived in the U.S.

Latinx Communities are often portrayed through the lens of illegality or threat, reducing millions of people to immigration status instead of recognizing identities rooted in long histories, cultures, and civic contributions.

Muslim and Arab Americans are frequently associated with danger, particularly after 9/11, despite the overwhelming diversity and peaceful lives of these communities.

Jewish Americans contend with stereotypes that simultaneously portray them as weak victims and powerful conspirators, two deeply contradictory but persistent narratives used to justify exclusion or violence.

LGBTQ+ Communities have long been cast as immoral, unhealthy, or socially dangerous. These narratives justified historical criminalization and contemporary discrimination.

People With Disabilities have been framed as burdens or objects of sympathy rather than independent individuals deserving of rights, access, and autonomy.

Rural Communities are often dismissed as uneducated, resistant to progress, or socially regressive, ignoring the economic extraction and political neglect that shape rural conditions.

How Narrative Harm Shapes Identity

When harmful narratives dominate, people internalize them. They shape how children see themselves and what adults believe to be possible. A narrative can constrict ambition, limit belonging, or reduce a person's confidence in their own potential.

These stories become psychological boundaries. Even when they are not spoken aloud, they influence how people interpret their experiences: whether they feel welcome in certain spaces, whether they expect fairness, and whether they imagine themselves as leaders, innovators, or full participants in civic life.

When a community is consistently portrayed as deficient, people may begin to believe they deserve less than others. This is how stories become infrastructure—not just influencing policy but shaping the internal worlds of individuals.

Minimal Checklist: Spotting Harmful Narratives

A narrative is likely harmful if it does any of the following:

- reduces a group to one trait
- ignores structural causes
- treats the community as a problem

Short, simple, and sufficient.

Minimal Craft Guidance: Avoiding Harm

Stronger narratives:

- reflect community-defined identity
- restore historical and social context
- show diversity and agency

Reflection Activity

Recall a narrative you grew up hearing about your own community. Identify what part of that story was incomplete or distorted, and write one paragraph correcting it using context, history, and lived experience.

Anecdote: When One Story Changed Everything

Janelle spent her childhood hearing the same message: her community was broken. Teachers repeated it. Television reinforced it. Politicians used it as a talking point. The story framed people like her as passive and dependent, defined more by their struggles than their strengths.

Everything shifted the day an organizer from her neighborhood spoke at her school. Instead of describing dysfunction, he talked about informal childcare networks, cultural traditions kept alive by elders, and the creativity people used to survive when institutions failed them. For the first time, Janelle saw her community reflected through a lens of competence and courage, not deficiency. That experience revealed a powerful truth: **if a narrative can be constructed, it can be reconstructed.**

> This is the work of rewriting narrative frames, correcting distortions, restoring humanity, and re-centering the truth communities know about themselves.

What It Means to Rewrite a Narrative

Rewriting a narrative does not mean creating an idealized version of reality. It means telling the whole truth, not the narrow slice that historically benefited outsiders or institutions. It is the process of restoring context where it has been stripped away, and complexity where it has been flattened.

It is the process of restoring context where it has been stripped away, and complexity where it has been flattened.

A rewritten narrative exposes how harmful stories were created in the first place: what political needs they served, what fears they activated, and what histories they erased. More importantly, rewritten narratives shift focus from blame to understanding, from stigma to possibility, from individual failure to structural realities.

This process also restores agency. It stops presenting communities as passive objects and instead recognizes them as active interpreters and creators of meaning. People are no longer cast as symbols of decline but as authors of their own stories.

How Communities Rewrite Their Narratives

Every community covered in your Cultural Competency content has challenged the stories imposed on them. Below is your material transformed into a narrative-style summary with minimal bullets.

Indigenous Nations

Indigenous communities counter the "vanishing race" myth by asserting sovereignty, revitalizing languages, and demonstrating that their cultures are not relics but living, evolving systems. Their stories highlight survival, political strength, and continuity despite centuries of erasure.

Black America

Black communities challenge narratives of pathology by exposing the structural roots of inequality and foregrounding traditions of intellectual innovation, organizing, artistry, and resistance. They rewrite frames that once cast them as problems and instead situate themselves as central builders of American democracy.

Asian Americans

Asian Americans dismantle the "model minority" myth by revealing its role in dividing minority groups and hiding real disparities. Their counter-stories emphasize diversity, histories of exclusion, and growing political leadership, showing that they are neither silent nor monolithic.

Latinx Communities

Latinx communities rewrite narratives of illegality by centering multigenerational presence, cultural richness, and civic power. Their stories foreground students, workers, artists, and organizers who have redefined what leadership and belonging look like across the country.

Muslim and Arab Americans

These communities disrupt narratives that equate Muslim identity with danger. Their counter-narratives highlight compassion, scholarship, family life, and community-building, challenging decades of political and media distortion.

Jewish Americans

Jewish counter-narratives resist portrayals that lock their identity into victimhood or suspicion. They emphasize cultural contribution, resilience, and historical continuity, reclaiming a nuanced and self-defined identity.

LGBTQ+ Communities

LGBTQ+ narratives reject portrayals of immorality and deviance. They tell stories of joy, chosen family, creativity, and political organizing, reframing LGBTQ+ identity as a source of strength and social transformation.

People With Disabilities

People with disabilities rewrite narratives that portray them as burdens by claiming visibility, leadership, independence, and rights. Their stories show disability as a political identity, not a personal tragedy, laying the groundwork for the ADA and ongoing fights for accessibility.

Rural Communities

Rural people challenge portrayals of backwardness by highlighting innovation, multiracial histories, and community problem-solving. Their narratives show structural neglect, not personal failure, as the root of many challenges.

Why Narrative Rewriting Works

Rewriting narratives works because it reshapes both internal identity and public imagination. Psychology has long shown that people act on the stories they believe about themselves. When harmful narratives dominate, hope shrinks. When counter-narratives take root, agency expands.

Hope theory describes this through two components:

- **Agency:** the belief that one can act.
- **Pathways:** the belief that paths to action exist.

A powerful counter-narrative activates both. It restores belief in the self and reveals pathways previously hidden behind stigma and distortion. Communities begin to see themselves not as exceptions who somehow "overcome," but as participants in a broader story of resilience, courage, and capacity.

> This is why narrative rewriting is not simply cultural work—it is civic work. It affects policy, public allocation, and collective vision.

Cultural Competency as a Method for Narrative Repair

Cultural competency is not politeness or sensitivity training. It is the discipline of understanding histories, power, and identity in a way that prevents narrative harm and supports narrative accuracy. It requires recognizing the origins of dominant narratives, the structures that sustain them, and the lived experiences they distort.

Culturally competent practitioners ask:

- Where did this story come from?
- Who benefits from it?
- What truths does it ignore?
- What structures shaped it?
- How do the people in this community define themselves?

The goal is not to create flattering narratives, but truthful ones. Narrative repair relies on precision, humility, and sustained engagement with communities, not assumptions.

Rewriting Narratives

- Does it restore context?
- Does it show agency?
- Does it include structural factors?

Reflection Activity

Write a short paragraph rewriting a narrative you've encountered in your own life. Focus on adding context, complexity, and agency.

Case Study: Rewriting the Narrative of Disability

Stories about disability have long been shaped by pity, charity, and assumptions of dependency. People with disabilities were often portrayed as objects of care rather than individuals with agency, knowledge, and political power. These portrayals weren't just insulting—they shaped law, policy, and everyday treatment. For decades, disabled people were segregated in institutions, denied education, excluded from public life, and treated as incapable of self-determination.

But the disability community rebuilt its narrative from the ground up. They replaced the story of "burden" with a story of rights, dignity, and collective action. This shift became one of the most important narrative transformations in U.S. civil rights history.

Historical Roots of the Harmful Narrative

For most of the 20th century, society told a single story about disabled people: that they were tragic, helpless, and in need of protection. This story appeared everywhere—textbooks, medical systems, charity campaigns, and government institutions. It described disability as a personal failure, a medical defect, or a private sorrow to be managed quietly.

The consequences were severe. Many disabled people were forced into institutions, denied jobs, blocked from public transportation, and separated from mainstream education. The physical environment—buildings, schools, sidewalks, buses—was designed as if disabled people did not exist. The narrative made exclusion sound natural.

The story was wrong, but it was powerful. It defined disabled people by what they could not do, rather than by who they were or how society had failed to accommodate them.

The Turning Point: A Community Rejects the Old Story

By the 1970s and 1980s, disabled activists began rejecting the paternalistic story imposed on them. They reframed disability not as an individual defect but as a social and political issue, one caused by inaccessible environments, discriminatory laws, and social assumptions.

This shift was radical. It meant:

- disability was not a tragedy
- exclusion was not inevitable
- the problem was not the person, it was the system

> Disabled activists insisted on being seen as full citizens. They demanded rights, not charity, equality, not sympathy. They fought for legal protections, public access, and recognition of disability as a natural part of human diversity. Their message was simple but transformative: "**Nothing about us, without us.**"

The Capitol Crawl: A Narrative Shift in Motion

One of the most powerful moments in this narrative transformation took place on March 12, 1990. Activists arrived at the steps of the U.S. Capitol to demand passage of the Americans with Disabilities Act (ADA). Many had been told their entire lives that disability made them powerless.

Instead, they showed the country a different story.

Dozens of disabled people left their wheelchairs and mobility devices and crawled up the Capitol steps using their hands, arms, and bodies. Their message was unmistakable: it was not their bodies that held them back, but a country that refused to build an accessible world.

This act did more than protest, it shattered the public narrative of passivity and dependency. It showed disabled people as leaders, strategists, and agents of change. The image contrasted sharply with the pity-based narratives Americans were accustomed to seeing.

The Capitol Crawl made it impossible to ignore the injustice of inaccessibility. Within months, the ADA passed.

Narratives became law.

How the New Narrative Reshaped Public Life

The ADA established civil rights protections in employment, transportation, public buildings, and communication access. But the deeper change was cultural. By challenging the story society believed about them, disabled people forced institutions to change as well.

The new narrative emphasized:

- autonomy
- political power
- everyday leadership
- community identity
- the right to participate fully in public life

This wasn't simply a story shift, it was a redefinition of disability itself, from private misfortune to collective civil rights.

The ADA codified this understanding, requiring society to adapt rather than expecting disabled people to disappear into the margins.

What This Case Study Shows About Narrative Power

The disability rights movement demonstrates that rewriting a narrative can transform institutions, laws, and public behavior. It proves that stories are not symbolic, they are structural. Before accessibility ramps, there had to be a narrative that said disabled people belonged in public spaces. Before anti-discrimination laws, there had to be a narrative that recognized disabled people as full citizens.

This case reveals a pattern:

1. A harmful narrative shapes public assumptions.
2. Those assumptions shape policy.
3. A counter-narrative challenges the old story.
4. Public imagination shifts.
5. Institutions change to match the new story.

Narrative change becomes civic change.

Minimal Checklist: Lessons From the Case Study

- Narratives influence who is seen as deserving of rights.
- Changing the story can change the law.
- Communities must be the authors of their own narratives.

Reflection Activity

Think of a group discussed in this chapter. What narrative reshaped their political or social standing? What action, event, or cultural moment served as the "Capitol Crawl" in their story?

STORY GENERATION, INTERVIEWING & SOURCE HANDLING

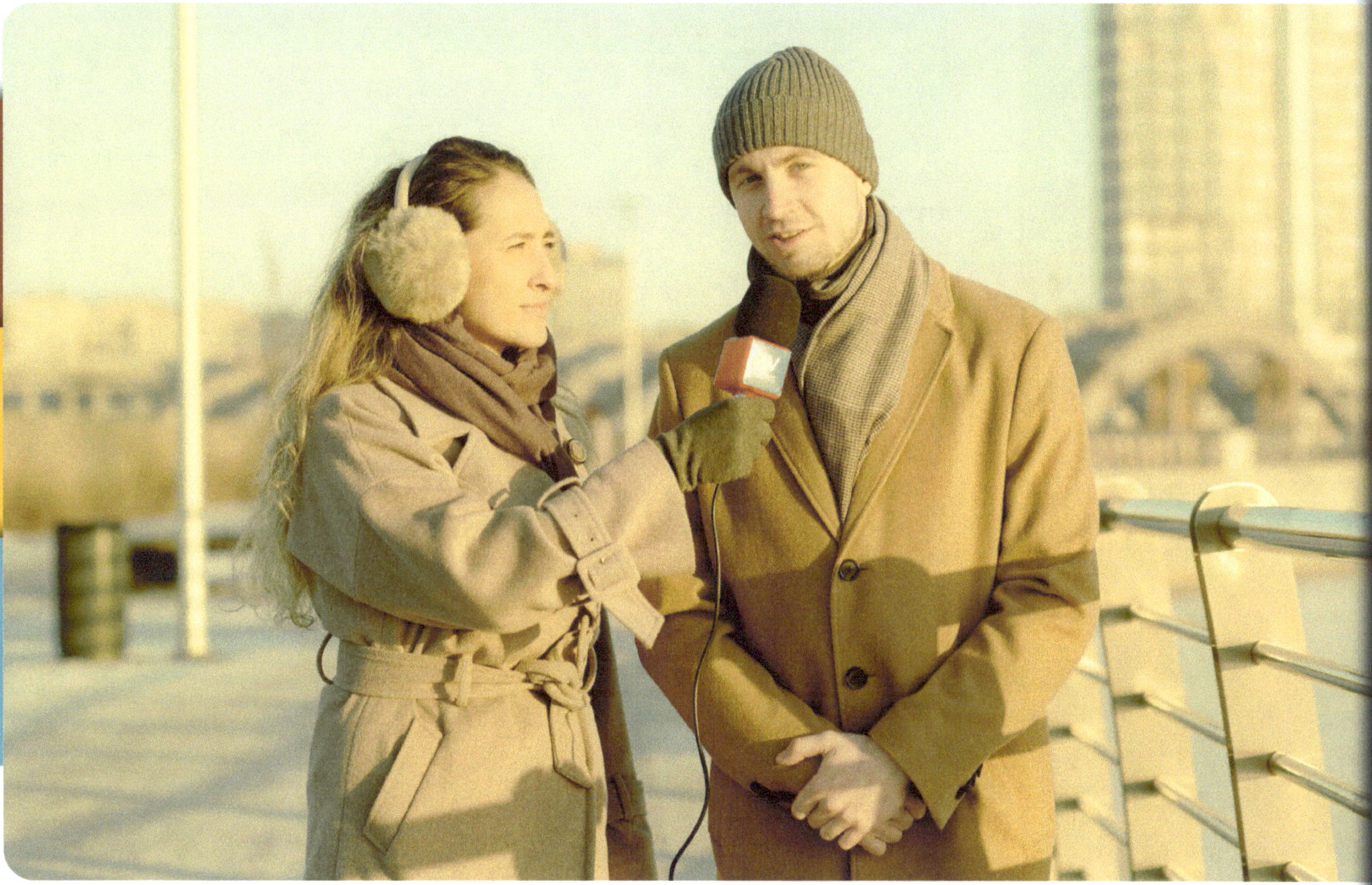

PLACED-BASED LEARNING SERIES

Overview

Every strong piece of journalism begins with two interconnected skills: the ability to recognize a story worth telling and the ability to interview sources in ways that uncover truth, nuance, and context. This chapter brings together the foundations of journalism and reporting to help students move from curiosity to publishable reporting.

Story generation is not simply about inspiration. It is a disciplined process that requires observation, listening, community awareness, and a deep understanding of what information the public needs. Students will learn how to identify potential stories in their everyday environments, how to transform tips into clear, actionable pitches, and how to evaluate whether an idea serves an audience meaningfully.

From there, the chapter transitions into interviewing, the skill that gives journalism its human depth and factual foundation. Good interviews do not happen by accident. They require preparation, structure, ethical decision-making, and an understanding of power dynamics between reporter and source. Students will learn how to craft effective questions, guide conversations with clarity and empathy, establish trust, and handle sensitive or high-pressure interviews responsibly.

Ethical quoting and source accuracy form another essential part of this chapter. In this chapter, we will explore how to quote responsibly, how to avoid distortions or selective editing, and how to uphold the integrity of each source's voice. The chapter also introduces key legal standards related to interviewing and source handling, including defamation, consent, privacy concerns, and policies involving

Overview...

minors or vulnerable individuals. These are not abstract rules, they shape every decision a journalist makes when gathering and using information.

A case study on "interviewing under pressure" demonstrates how these skills come together in real-world reporting, highlighting the challenges journalists face when navigating tense, emotional, or time-sensitive situations. Throughout the chapter, students will also encounter practical activities, checklists, and reflective exercises designed to strengthen their ability to generate stories, conduct ethical interviews, and handle sources with care.

Section 5.1: Finding Story Ideas & Turning Tips into Pitches

Good reporting begins long before the first interview is scheduled or the first sentence is written. It begins with the ability to recognize a meaningful story. Strong journalists learn to see potential stories not just in breaking news or dramatic events, but in everyday patterns, overlooked issues, unanswered questions, and structural tensions. This capacity, story generation, is both a creative habit and a disciplined craft.

We are surrounded by stories all the time. The challenge is learning to observe the world with curiosity and intention. Some stories emerge from formal channels: public meetings, press releases, community announcements. Others surface quietly through small observations: a crowded bus stop, a classroom debate, a neighborhood dispute, an unexpected closure, or a sudden shift in community mood. Journalists must train themselves to notice these signals and consider whether they point toward a public need.

Strong journalists learn to see potential stories not just in breaking news or dramatic events, but in everyday patterns, overlooked issues, unanswered questions, and structural tensions.

This section explores how to generate meaningful story ideas, how to evaluate their potential, and how to transform them into clear, credible pitches that editors and readers can understand.

Anecdote: The Story Hidden in Plain Sight

During her first semester reporting, a student named Laila walked past the same hallway bulletin board every day. She never paid attention to it, it was cluttered with flyers for tutoring, clubs, and campus events. One afternoon, while waiting for class, she noticed a small, printed sheet announcing that the university had changed its emergency grant process for students facing housing or food insecurity.

At first, she didn't think much of it. But later, she wondered: Why had the university changed the process? Did students know? More importantly, were they struggling to access support because of the new rules?

When Laila started asking questions, she discovered that the new process—supposedly designed to increase efficiency, had accidentally created delays. Students were waiting weeks for emergency funds meant to be issued within days. Some had been forced to borrow money, take on extra jobs, or skip meals while waiting for approval.

A story that seemed insignificant became a meaningful piece of journalism once she looked closely. What made it a story was not the flyer itself, but the tension behind it: the gap between policy intention and student experience.

This illustrates a fundamental truth: stories often hide in the background of everyday life. Journalists must train themselves to notice what others overlook.

Where Story Ideas Come From

Story ideas rarely appear fully formed. They often emerge from fragments, observations, concerns, complaints, patterns, or questions that linger.

Common sources of story ideas include:

1. Everyday observation

Noticing small changes, inconsistencies, or patterns in the environment: a long line outside a campus office, a closed local business, a sudden shift in bus schedules, or new signage appearing without explanation.

2. Conversations with community members

Students, neighbors, parents, local officials, workers, and community organizers are often the first to identify emerging issues.

3. Institutional decisions

Policies, budgets, resolutions, new programs, or administrative actions frequently affect people's lives in ways that warrant deeper explanation.

4. Public data and records

Budget spreadsheets, meeting minutes, inspection records, enrollment statistics, and court filings contain story material waiting to be uncovered.

5. Social media patterns

Repeated complaints, questions, or rumors online often reflect underlying community concerns.

6. Gaps in previous reporting

Sometimes the story is what media outlets *failed* to cover, missing voices, unexamined consequences, or lack of context.

7. Tips from sources

A tip is not a story, but it may be the spark that leads to one. Journalists must learn to evaluate and verify tips without assuming they are accurate.

These sources reflect the central idea in JOU 101: story generation starts with active awareness. Students should approach the world with curiosity, asking not just *what happened* but *why it matters*.

Evaluating Which Ideas Become Stories

Not every idea is strong enough to become a full story. Journalists must learn to evaluate potential stories using key questions:

- **Who is affected?**
  A story with broad or deep impact is more valuable than one affecting very few.
- **Is there tension or conflict?**
  A story is stronger when there is a question, gap, contradiction, pressure, or change.
- **Is there a public need for information?**
  Journalism serves the public; a strong story addresses a real need.
- **Is the issue timely?**
  Some stories matter because they are unfolding now or because the window for understanding is short.
- **Does the idea reveal or explain something new?**
  Journalists add value by providing insight—not repeating what everyone already knows.
- **Is it verifiable?**
  Stories must be backed by evidence, not speculation.
- **Are key voices accessible?**
  If sources refuse to speak and records are unavailable, the story may be impossible to complete fairly.

Ideas that meet these criteria often have the strongest potential.

Turning Ideas into Publishable Pitches

A pitch is a bridge between observation and reporting. It tells the editor what the story is, why it matters, and how the reporting will proceed. Students often confuse pitches with topics, but the two are not the same.

A **topic** is broad: "food insecurity," "mental health," "traffic issues," "campus renovations."

A **pitch** is precise: "The university's emergency grant delays are causing students experiencing housing insecurity to wait weeks for funds intended to provide same-day support. Students and staff describe confusion, miscommunication, and gaps in policy implementation."

A strong pitch includes:

1. **The central issue**
   What the story is about in one clear sentence.
2. **Why it matters**
   Who is affected and why the public should care.
3. **Evidence of the problem**
   Anecdotes, observations, or early reporting that points to deeper issues.
4. **Reporting plan**
   Key sources you will interview, records you will seek, and methods of verification.
5. **Audience angle**
   How the story serves public needs, not just news-cycle interest.

> A pitch is not a script. It is a roadmap. It shows that the journalist understands the issue, has done background research, and has a plan to pursue the story responsibly.

From Tips to Verified Stories

Journalists must learn to treat tips as starting points, not conclusions. A tip might be:

- an email from a frustrated student
- a rumor circulating online
- a parent's complaint
- a questionable photo

- a claim made in a meeting
- a whisper about wrongdoing

Tips can be useful, but they are not facts. The path from tip to story usually follows three steps:

1. Verify the tip independently

Seek documentation, multiple sources, or observational evidence.

2. Identify the real issue

Sometimes the tip is the symptom, not the story.

3. Evaluate whether it serves the public

A tip becomes a story only if it reveals something meaningful for readers.

The discipline of verification protects both the journalist and the audience from misinformation.

Examples from Real Reporting

Positive Example: Turning a Tip into a Systemic Story

A local reporter received a tip that a single restaurant was mislabeling food allergens. After investigating, she learned that the city's entire food inspection system was understaffed, leading to unsafe conditions citywide. The tip led to a broader, more impactful story.

Harmful Example: Publishing Without Verifying a Tip

During an election, a newsroom published a viral rumor about malfunctioning voting machines without verification. The information was false and eroded public trust. The error came from treating a tip as a fact.

Student Example: The Hidden Cost of Course Materials

A student overheard peers complaining about rising textbook prices. After investigating, he discovered inconsistent pricing between bookstore locations and online versions. The pitch became a data-supported story with real impact.

Craft Guidance: Building a Habit of Curiosity

The strongest student journalists build routines that encourage curiosity.

Helpful habits include:

- reading local board agendas weekly
- walking different areas of campus or town to observe changes
- asking "why?" when something seems unusual
- keeping a notebook of small observations
- talking with people outside one's own social circle
- attending public meetings or forums
- browsing public data sets or city dashboards

These habits transform daily life into a source of potential stories.

Light Checklist: Evaluating a Story Idea

- Does this story affect real people?
- Is there tension, contradiction, or unanswered questions?
- Is the issue timely or emerging?
- Can it be verified with evidence?
- Is the idea original, or can it be framed in an original way?
- Does it serve an audience's needs?
- Is it feasible with available time and resources?

Reflection Activity

Identify three potential story ideas from your campus or community. For each idea, write:

1. What makes the idea interesting
2. Who is affected
3. What questions remain unanswered
4. How you would verify the central claims
5. How you would pitch the story to an editor

Choose one and turn it into a full pitch based on the guidelines in this section.

Section 5.2: Interviewing Techniques, Structure & Ethical Source Handling

Interviewing is one of the most fundamental skills in journalism. It is where information becomes human, where facts gain nuance, and where complexity emerges through the voices of the people most affected by an issue. Good interviews reveal not only what happened, but how it felt, why it matters, and where the deeper tensions lie. Yet strong interviewing is not simply a conversation; it is a structured, intentional process grounded in preparation, clear communication, and ethical responsibility.

> This section explores how journalists design, conduct, and navigate interviews; how they manage source relationships with integrity; how they avoid manipulation or selective editing; and how legal and ethical standards shape every step of the process. Interviewing is both a craft and a discipline, and this section helps students build confidence in both.

Anecdote: The Interview That Went Sideways

Sofia believed she had prepared well for her interview with a high-ranking university administrator about changes to mental-health services. She had three pages of questions, most of them detailed, policy-focused, and technical. But the moment the interview began, the administrator took control of the conversation. He spoke in rehearsed statements, offered long monologues filled with institutional jargon, and brushed aside student concerns.

Sofia left feeling frustrated. She had barely asked any of her questions, and the answers she received were vague. Her editor later explained that she had entered the interview without a clear strategy. Instead of preparing *questions*, she needed to prepare a *structure*, a roadmap that allowed her to guide the conversation, redirect when necessary, and stay grounded in the story's purpose.

This experience taught Sofia what all strong reporters eventually learn: interviews are not passive exchanges. They require planning, listening, boundaries, and confidence.

Preparing for the Interview: The Work Happens Before You Arrive

Good interviews start long before the first question is asked. Preparation equips journalists to recognize meaningful detail, challenge unclear statements, and avoid being misled, intentionally or unintentionally.

Preparation includes:

1. Understanding the issue deeply. Reporters should know enough background information to ask informed questions and avoid wasting time on information already available.

2. Identifying what you truly need to learn. Interviews are most effective when guided by specific goals: clarifying contradictions, understanding lived experience, explaining processes, or uncovering new angles.

3. Researching the person being interviewed. Knowing a source's background, prior statements, and role allows the reporter to ask sharper questions.

4. Planning the interview structure. Good interviews often follow a sequence: open-ended questions to establish comfort, focused questions to probe specifics, and clarifying questions to confirm accuracy.

Prepared journalists enter interviews with confidence and clarity, not with pages of disconnected questions.

Structuring Effective Interviews

A well-structured interview helps maintain focus, encourage depth, and build trust. Students often rely too heavily on scripted lists of questions, which can limit spontaneity and prevent deeper insights. Instead, interviews should follow a logical flow that allows for flexibility while maintaining direction.

A strong interview often includes:

1. Openers that build rapport

Start with accessible questions that allow the source to speak in their own voice: "Can you tell me what happened from your perspective?" "How long have you been involved in this issue?"

2. Exploratory questions

These help uncover the deeper context, emotions, and stakes: "What was the most challenging part of this process for you?" "What do you wish people understood?"

3. Clarifying questions

These cut through vague language and ensure accuracy: "When you say the process was confusing, what specifically made it confusing?" "Can you give me an example?"

4. Verification questions

Journalists must confirm details, timelines, and names to prevent errors.

5. Accountability questions

When speaking with officials or people in positions of power, questions must be direct and precise: "Why was this decision made?" "What evidence supports this claim?" "What is your response to people who feel harmed by this policy?"

6. Closing questions

These allow sources to add essential details the journalist may have overlooked: "Is there anything important I didn't ask?" "What should people know that they often misunderstand?"

This structure keeps interviews balanced, human, factual, and focused.

The Art of Listening: Where Interviews Truly Happen

Strong interviewing depends more on listening than on talking. Journalists must tune into what sources say, how they say it, and what they do *not* say.

Listening allows reporters to:

- notice inconsistencies
- pick up on emotional cues
- follow promising threads
- abandon prewritten questions when better ones emerge
- ask follow-ups that reveal deeper truth

Some of the best interviews come from simple, attentive follow-ups: "What happened next?" "What do you mean by that?" "Why do you think that is?"

Listening is also how journalists avoid projecting assumptions or misinterpreting a source's meaning. The interview becomes a dialogue, not an interrogation.

Power Dynamics: Who Holds Control in an Interview?

Not all interviews are equal. Power dynamics shape the interaction. Interviews with officials, CEOs, police, university administrators, or spokespeople require assertiveness and preparation, they may deflect, minimize, or redirect. Interviews with vulnerable individuals, trauma survivors, minors, marginalized groups, require sensitivity and care.

Strong journalists adapt their approach to match the power imbalance:

- With **officials** → ask clear, direct, verifiable questions.
- With **community members** → prioritize comfort, clarity, and safety.
- With **people in crisis** → avoid pressing for emotional detail; allow pauses.
- With **minors or vulnerable adults** → follow legal and ethical guidelines carefully.

A good interviewer adjusts, not manipulates.

Ethical Quoting & Source Accuracy

Ethical quoting is central to trusted and reliable news. Quotes must reflect exactly what a source said, not what the journalist *remembers* or *interprets*. Reporters often unintentionally distort quotes by:

- "cleaning up" grammar to sound more polished
- compressing long explanations into sharper soundbites
- replacing nuance with dramatic phrasing
- paraphrasing but presenting it as a direct quote

These errors can misrepresent sources and damage trust.

Ethical quoting requires:

- checking quotes against recordings or notes
- clarifying when meaning is unclear
- avoiding selective editing that skews context
- preserving tone and intent
- using ellipses sparingly and transparently

If a quote is confusing, the journalist should ask the source to restate the idea during the interview, not "fix" it later.

Avoiding Manipulation & Selective Editing

Journalists must not shape interviews to fit a predetermined narrative. Selective editing, choosing only the parts of a source's statement that support a point while removing nuance, creates misleading stories.

Selective editing includes:

- removing context that explains meaning
- ignoring contradictory statements
- framing quotes to suggest blame or certainty that did not exist
- using emotional clips to exaggerate conflict
- presenting moments out of chronological order

Responsible editing preserves the truth rather than crafting drama.

Legal Standards Every Interviewer Must Know

Interviewing is shaped not just by ethics, but by law. Students must understand legal boundaries to protect themselves, their sources, and their publication.

The essentials include:

Defamation

Reporters must avoid false statements that harm a person's reputation. Verification is the first line of defense.

Consent

In some states, recording interviews requires two-party consent. Journalists must know local laws and always disclose recordings.

Privacy

Publishing private facts, especially about minors or trauma survivors, can lead to legal and ethical consequences.

Minors

Interviewing minors often requires parental consent, especially in sensitive stories or institutional settings.

Public vs. private settings

Expectations of privacy differ. Interviews in public spaces are legally safer than in private settings.

Understanding these standards prevents mistakes that can jeopardize a story, or a publication.

Case Study: Interviewing Under Pressure

During wildfires in northern California, a young reporter named Jordan was dispatched to interview families who had just lost their homes. The situation was chaotic: smoke in the air, people crying, officials shouting instructions.

Jordan's first instinct was to ask questions immediately. But he paused. He realized people were overwhelmed, frightened, and processing trauma. Instead of forcing interviews, he approached gently:

"Is now an okay time to talk? It's completely fine to say no."

Some said yes. Others couldn't speak. Jordan respected each answer.

> When people did open up, Jordan asked simple, grounding questions: "What happened?" "What do you need right now?" "Is there someone you're trying to reach?"

He avoided pressing for emotional details. He checked facts later with officials. He allowed silence. He did not use quotes spoken in confusion or shock.

The resulting story was not dramatic, but it was accurate, humane, and deeply powerful. It earned praise because it reflected care, not exploitation.

Jordan modeled exactly what students must learn: interviewing under pressure requires emotional intelligence, restraint, and integrity.

Light Checklist: Ethical Interviewing

- Am I prepared with background knowledge?
- Do my questions reflect curiosity, not assumptions?
- Am I listening more than speaking?
- Did I verify quotes carefully?
- Am I avoiding selective editing?
- Did I treat the source with respect and fairness?
- Am I aware of legal and ethical boundaries?

Reflection Activity

Choose a real person affected by a policy, campus issue, or community concern. Draft 8–10 interview questions using the structure in this section: rapport, exploration, clarification, verification, and closing. Then write a short reflection explaining how you would adapt your approach depending on the source's level of power, vulnerability, or lived experience.

Section 5.3: Legal Standards, Accuracy, and Interviewing Under Pressure (Case Study)

Interviews may seem simple, two people talking, but the decisions a journalist makes during, before, and after the conversation can carry significant legal, ethical, and narrative consequences. This section explores the legal framework surrounding interviews, the obligation to be accurate and fair, and the realities of conducting interviews under pressure. Working within these standards protects journalists, strengthens reporting, and builds trust between newsrooms and the communities they serve.

The goal is not to intimidate students with rules, but to equip them with the confidence to make clear, responsible decisions. Good journalism thrives on precision, respect, and accountability.

Understanding the Legal Landscape of Interviews

Journalists operate in a legal environment shaped by state law, federal guidelines, and long-standing case precedents. Students often believe legal concerns only arise during high-stakes investigations, but even routine interviews have legal implications.

Here are the areas every reporter, even a student reporter, must understand:

1. Defamation: The Most Common Legal Risk

Defamation occurs when false statements harm a person's reputation. It includes:

- **libel** (written)
- **slander** (spoken)

> Journalists avoid defamation by verifying facts thoroughly, avoiding assumptions, and quoting accurately. Importantly:

- *Truth is a complete defense.*
- *Opinion is protected if it is clearly framed as opinion, not fact.*
- *Public officials and public figures must prove "actual malice."*
- *Private individuals require only negligence.*

Students must remember: accusations, insinuations, or interpretations without evidence can create legal problems, even in small publications.

2. Consent & Recording Laws

The rules vary by location:

- **One-party consent states** allow a journalist to record as long as *one person in the conversation* consents (often the journalist themself).
- **Two-party consent states** require that *everyone involved* knows the conversation is being recorded.

Ethically and professionally, best practice is simple: **Always tell sources when you are recording.**

This builds trust and avoids complications later.

3. Privacy & Intrusion

Even in public-service reporting, journalists must respect privacy. Legal claims arise when reporters:

- disclose highly sensitive private facts
- use hidden recording devices in private spaces
- publish medical or academic information without consent
- show faces of minors in sensitive situations without permission

Journalists may cover public spaces freely, but private spaces require caution and documented permission.

4. Interviewing Minors

Minors deserve extra protection. Ethical guidelines, reinforced by JOU 102, include:

- obtaining parental or guardian consent for interviews
- avoiding questions that could distress or confuse minors
- never quoting minors in criminal or deeply sensitive contexts without clear approval
- protecting minors' identities when safety is at risk

Minors should never be pushed into discussing trauma or controversy simply because they are articulate.

5. Public vs. Private Settings

Legal risk shifts depending on location:

- **Public places** (sidewalks, parks, campus quads): interviews and photos are generally safe.
- **Semi-public places** (schools, hospitals, shelters): require institutional rules and permissions.
- **Private homes:** require explicit consent.

> Knowing these boundaries prevents misunderstandings and protects journalists legally.

Accuracy: The Non-Negotiable Standard

Accuracy is not only an ethical obligation, it is also a legal safeguard. Courts consistently emphasize that journalists who demonstrate diligence, transparency, and verification are far less likely to face successful legal challenges.

Accuracy practices include:

- verifying all factual claims with multiple sources
- double-checking spellings, dates, titles, and numbers
- reviewing quotes against audio recordings
- clarifying ambiguous statements
- confirming timelines with multiple witnesses
- avoiding assumptions or interpretations not supported by evidence

Accuracy builds credibility and strengthens the narrative. Errors, especially small ones, signal carelessness, which can undermine trust in the entire story.

Avoiding Selective Editing, Misrepresentation & Coercion

Ethical source handling means avoiding manipulative techniques that distort meaning. These actions may not be illegal, but they violate journalistic standards:

- taking quotes out of context
- cropping interviews to exaggerate emotion or anger
- omitting parts of a statement that complicate the narrative
- leading questions designed to prompt specific answers
- pressuring sources into on-the-record statements
- editing video or audio to change the meaning or timeline

Even subtle manipulations can mislead audiences. Journalists must represent people honestly, without embellishing or stripping away nuance.

When Sources Try to Manipulate the Interview

Manipulation goes both ways. Some sources, especially officials, PR representatives, administrators, or corporate spokespeople, may:

- avoid answering questions
- use rehearsed talking points
- redirect the conversation
- misstate facts
- imply consequences if quoted directly
- attempt to negotiate which topics are "off-limits"

Strong interviewers maintain control by:

- returning calmly to the question
- requesting clarification
- pressing for specifics
- asking for evidence to support claims
- documenting all exchanges
- keeping personal feelings out of the interaction

Journalists are not adversaries, but they must hold firm on public-interest questions.

Interviewing Under Pressure: An Extended Case Study

Earlier, Section 5.2 introduced a wildfire reporting anecdote. Here, we expand on the full scenario to illustrate the complexities and responsibilities of interviewing under pressure.

Context

During a series of rapidly spreading wildfires in northern California, a young journalist, Jordan, was assigned to gather firsthand accounts from displaced families arriving at an evacuation center. Emotions were high: people were exhausted, frightened, and unsure whether their homes still existed.

Challenge

Jordan needed quotes, scenes, and context. But immediate interviews risked retraumatizing survivors or capturing unreliable statements made under distress.

Approach

Jordan applied three principles central to good reporting:

1. Consent must be meaningful. He approached gently, "Would you be open to talking? If not, that's completely okay."

This allowed people to retain agency during a moment when much had been taken from them.

2. Questions must prioritize humanity. Instead of asking about loss, he asked grounding questions: "What happened?" Is everyone with you? "What do you need right now?"

These questions helped victims stay present and reduced the chance of misinterpretation.

3. Accuracy matters more than speed. Jordan avoided quoting statements made in panic. Instead, he later checked details:

- fire department logs
- evacuation notice
- official damage reports

He balanced emotional testimony with verified facts.

Outcome

The resulting story avoided sensationalism. It centered people's experiences while maintaining clarity and accuracy. Readers praised the coverage for being respectful, grounded, and compassionate, a reflection of strong interviewing practice under pressure.

Responsibility in High-Stakes Interviews

Whether the pressure comes from breaking news, controversial investigations, or emotionally sensitive situations, journalists must:

- remain calm
- make ethical decisions quickly
- avoid leading sources during distress
- reduce harm whenever possible
- prioritize accuracy over drama
- verify emotional testimony before publication
- remember that traumatized people cannot always provide reliable detail

These rules protect both the source and the integrity of the story.

Light Checklist: Legal & Ethical Safety in Interviews

- Did I obtain informed consent for the interview and recording?
- Have I verified all factual claims from the source?
- Did I avoid coercion, pressure, or manipulative framing?
- Did I treat minors and vulnerable people with heightened care?
- Am I aware of privacy concerns and state recording laws?
- Am I avoiding selective editing?
- Did I check quotes against original recordings?

Reflection Activity

Describe a scenario where an interview takes place under pressure—breaking news, emotional conflict, or institutional tension. Write how you would:

1. prepare for the interview
2. maintain ethical standards

3. handle recording and consent
4. protect accuracy
5. reduce harm to the source
6. maintain control of the conversation

This exercise will help reporters internalize interview ethics before facing real-world pressure.

CHAPTER 6

BUILDING STRONG STORY STRUCTURES & NARRATIVE FLOW

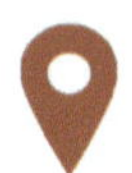

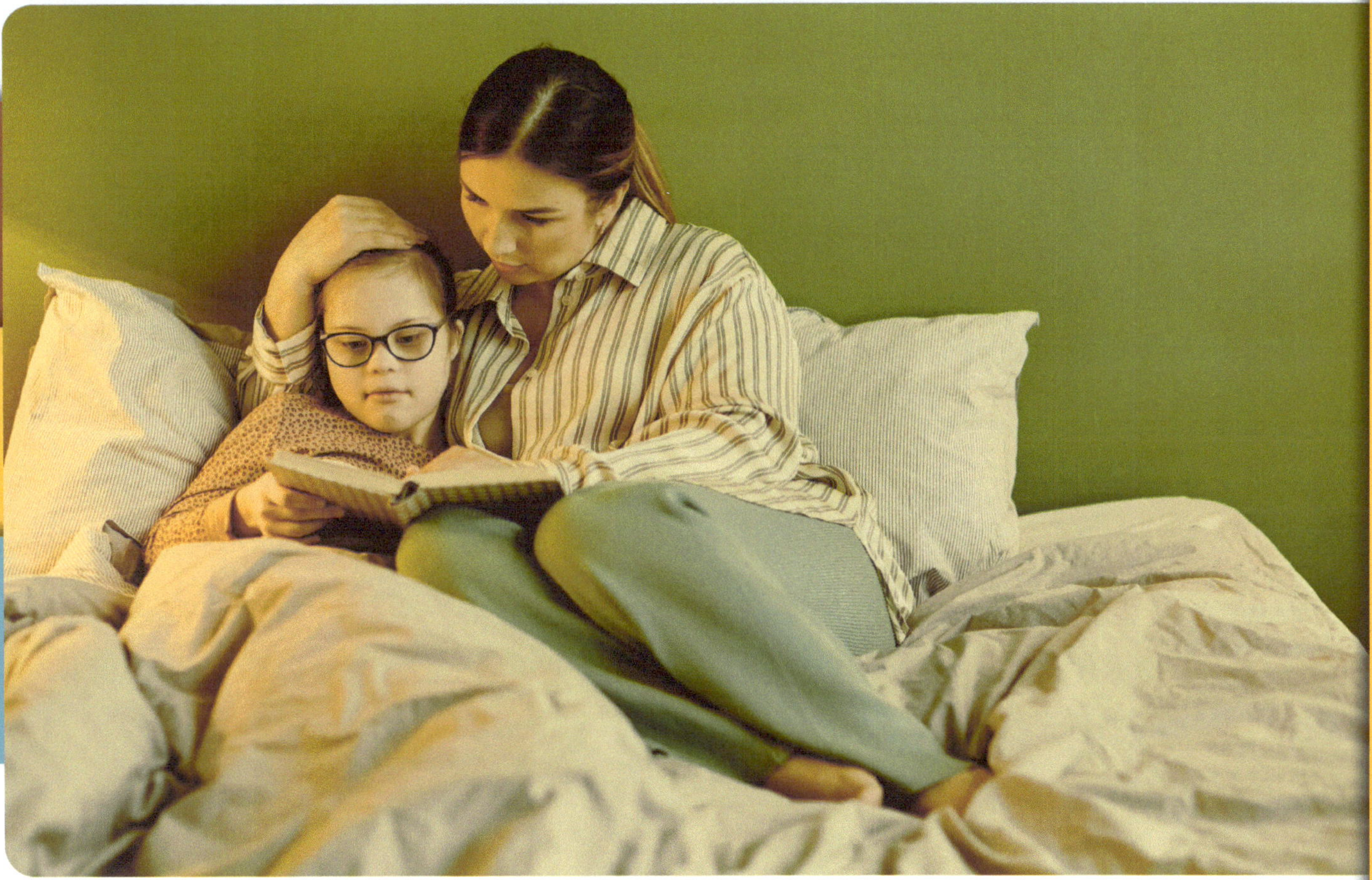

PLACED-BASED LEARNING SERIES

Overview

A well-constructed story is not an accident. It is the result of deliberate choices about structure, pacing, clarity, and movement. In journalism, especially feature writing, structure shapes meaning. It determines how readers understand an issue, connect with characters, follow complex information, and stay engaged from beginning to end. This chapter helps learners master the structural tools that every professional reporter needs.

Students will learn the major structures used across news and feature writing: the inverted pyramid, the hourglass, the narrative arc, the Q&A format, and the profile structure. Each structure serves a specific purpose, and choosing the right one is a strategic storytelling decision rooted in audience needs, narrative goals, and the nature of the reporting. Strong structure is not mechanical, it is intentional.

The chapter also explores what makes a strong lead and why some leads fail. Leads carry tremendous responsibility: they set tone, anchor the story, and guide readers into complex topics. Students will examine several lead types, understand when to use them, and practice identifying leads that fit the story's core purpose.

Beyond structure and leads, this chapter focuses on scene-building, pacing, and transitions, the techniques that breathe life into writing and help readers move through the narrative with clarity and momentum. These skills help students turn complex, technical, or "dry" topics into compelling stories anchored in human experience and accessible explanation.

Section 6.1: Mastering Story Structures: From News to Narrative

Story structure is the architecture of journalism. It shapes how information unfolds, guides readers through complex material, and determines whether a piece feels cohesive, compelling, or confusing. Strong reporting may uncover powerful facts, vivid scenes, and memorable voices, but without structure, those elements remain scattered. Structure is what turns raw material into narrative.

This section introduces the major structures taught in **JOU 201**, exploring how each one works, when it excels, and how journalists can match structure to story purpose. Whether writing breaking news or long-form features, reporters must choose a structure that supports clarity, reveals meaning, and respects audience needs.

Anecdote: Two Stories, One Problem. No Structure

During a feature-writing assignment, two students, Marcus and Dayna, were given the same reporting packet about a local entrepreneur rebuilding a bakery after a devastating fire. Both gathered excellent details: emotional interviews, financial records, descriptions of the fire, quotes from firefighters, and community reactions.

Marcus wrote a story that was technically accurate but emotionally flat. The paragraphs drifted, scenes appeared randomly, and readers could not tell what mattered most. Dayna, by contrast, crafted a narrative with focus. She opened with a vivid moment from the fire, transitioned into the bakery owner's long recovery, and introduced financial context at the right moment. Her story had flow, tension, and clarity.

The difference was not reporting ability, it was structure. Marcus piled information. Dayna constructed meaning.

This is the power of structure: it determines whether readers stay with a story or feel lost.

Why Structure Matters in Journalism

Structure affects every aspect of storytelling:

- **clarity:** helping readers follow complex events
- **engagement:** guiding the emotional and intellectual movement
- **credibility:** ensuring information unfolds logically
- **pace:** balancing fast information with slower, reflective moments
- **focus:** emphasizing the central tension without distraction

In JOU 201, structure is not treated as a formula but as a **toolbox**. Each structure has strengths and limitations. The journalist's job is to choose the right one, not the flashiest or the easiest, but the one that best fits the story's purpose.

The Inverted Pyramid: Prioritizing What Matters Most

The **inverted pyramid** is the backbone of traditional news writing. It places the most critical information at the top and arranges the rest in descending order of importance.

How it works

- The lead provides the essential facts (who, what, when, where, why, how).
- Key supporting details follow.
- Background and additional context appear near the end.

When to use it

- breaking news
- announcements
- event coverage

- public safety updates
- policy changes
- urgent community information

Why it matters

The structure ensures that even readers who only skim the first few paragraphs walk away informed. It also helps editors cut from the bottom without losing essential meaning.

Limitations

It is efficient but not emotional. It rarely works for character-driven or narrative features because it does not build suspense or deepen emotional connection.

The Hourglass: A Blend of News and Narrative

The **hourglass structure** begins with a traditional inverted pyramid lead but shifts into a chronological narrative after the essential facts are established.

How it works

1. Top: Key facts and summary lead (inverted pyramid).
2. Turn: The moment the story shifts, "but what happened next surprised them..."
3. Body: Narrative sequence, characters, scenes, dialogue.
4. End: Resolution or implication.

When to use it

- features based on breaking news
- crime or disaster stories with emotional movement
- investigations with both hard facts and narrative elements
- event reconstructions

Why it matters

It satisfies readers who want clear information *and* readers who enjoy story-driven flow.

Limitations

Requires enough narrative detail to sustain the chronological middle.

The Narrative Arc: Journalism That Reads Like a Story

Long-form features often rely on the **narrative arc**, which mirrors fiction but remains rooted in journalistic truth. It emphasizes characters, conflict, rising tension, and resolution.

Elements of the narrative arc

- scene-driven opening
- introduction of key characters
- central tension or conflict
- rising action or complications
- climax or turning point
- resolution or reflection

When to use it

- human-interest stories
- deep profiles
- long-form magazine features
- investigations centered on individuals
- community stories with movement and emotional stakes

Why it matters

Narrative arcs are immersive. They draw readers into the lived experience of a story and create emotional resonance.

Limitations

Requires strong reporting, rich scenes, and careful pacing. Not suitable for stories that need to deliver fast, factual updates.

The Q&A Format: Structured Transparency

The Q&A format presents the interview directly, allowing sources to speak in their own voice. It is not a shortcut; it is a strategic choice.

When to use it

- interviews with experts on complex topics
- conversations where the speaker's voice *is* the story
- rapid audience information (e.g., "What you need to know" interviews)
- profiles where personality and viewpoint matter most

Strengths

- clarity
- transparency
- minimal interpretation from the reporter
- direct access to a person's tone and perspective

Weaknesses

- requires clean, meaningful answers
- does not provide analysis unless paired with context
- fails when the source is vague, evasive, or disorganized

The Profile Structure: Portraits With Purpose

Profiles are not biographies. They are snapshots of a person that reveal something larger, an idea, a tension, a cultural moment, or a broader theme.

A strong profile structure includes:

- a vivid opening scene
- introduction of the central idea or theme
- background and formative experiences
- contradictions or complexities
- current challenges or achievements
- scenes that reveal personality
- a reflective or forward-looking ending

Profiles often blend narrative arc with thematic structure.

Choosing the Right Structure: It's a Strategic Decision

Structure should serve the story, not the other way around. Consider:

- **Who is the audience?**
  Are they seeking quick updates or immersive storytelling?
- **What is the central tension?**
  Is it a systemic issue, a character journey, or a chronological event?
- **What does the story need emotionally and intellectually?**
  Authority? Urgency? Depth? Suspense?
- **What does the material allow?**
  Do you have scenes? Characters? Movement? Data? Stakes?

Good reporters do not default to one structure out of habit. They choose intentionally

How Structure Supports Complex or "Dry" Topics

One of the most valuable skills in JOU 201 is learning how to turn technical or bureaucratic issues into engaging narratives. Structure helps by giving shape to complexity.

Examples:

- A data-heavy housing report might work best with an hourglass: key findings first, followed by a story of one tenant navigating the system.
- A policy shift might work with an inverted pyramid: essential information at the top, but with human context sprinkled in.
- A campus budget crisis might work with a narrative arc centered on the journey of one student or department affected by the cuts.

Structure is not merely stylistic; it is a clarity tool.

Scene, Movement & the Reader's Journey

Even within structured frameworks, journalists must think about how readers move through a story. Scenes, pacing, and flow help readers transition from fact to meaning, from moment to moment.

Structure provides the skeleton. Scenes and transitions provide the muscles and connective tissue.

you will explore these in detail in **Section 6.2**, but for now, it is important to understand that good structure:

- guides the reader's eye
- creates rhythm
- signals where to pay attention
- prevents confusion
- supports emotional resonance

> A well-structured story feels inevitable, like it could not have been told any other way.

Light Checklist: Identifying the Right Structure

- What is the story's core purpose?
- Who needs this information and in what form?
- Do I have scenes and characters?
- Do I need a fast lead or a narrative opening?
- Is the timeline essential?
- Does the structure create clarity or confusion?
- Does it match audience needs?

Reflection Activity

Choose one real or hypothetical story idea. Using the structures in this section, write three short pitches explaining how the story might be told:

1. as an inverted-pyramid news story
2. as an hourglass feature
3. as a narrative-arc story

Explain how the meaning, focus, and emotional tone shift with each structure.

Section 6.2: Leads, Scenes, Transitions & Narrative Movement

A story's structure provides the skeleton, but leads, scenes, pacing, and transitions determine how the reader *moves* through the story. These elements shape rhythm, emotion, clarity, and momentum. They show the difference between reporting that feels mechanical and reporting that feels alive. Even the best structure will fall flat if the writing itself does not guide the reader with intention. This section unpacks how effective leads draw readers in, how scenes bring stories to life, how pacing maintains attention, and how transitions build seamless flow from beginning to end.

Strong narrative movement doesn't happen by accident. It comes from deliberate choices that honor the story's purpose and respect the audience's time.

Anecdote: A Great Story Buried Under a Weak Beginning

During a feature-writing workshop, a student named Reese pitched an excellent story about an EMT trainee who froze during her first emergency call and later rebuilt her confidence through months of training. The reporting was rich: emotional interviews, vivid details from ambulance ride-alongs, and strong narrative tension.

But her first draft opened with three paragraphs of statistics about emergency response times.

The story's emotional core was buried beneath information that belonged later in the piece. When the instructor asked why she chose that lead, Reese said she felt "safer" starting with data, even though the human story was the reason she wanted to write the piece in the first place.

When she rewrote the lead to begin with the trainee stepping into a smoke-filled hallway for the first time, the story transformed. Suddenly readers cared. The narrative had energy. The structure found its heartbeat.

This is the lesson: **A lead is a doorway. Choose the right one.**

Understanding Leads: The First Promise You Make to Your Reader

The lead sets expectations, tone, pace, focus, and emotional weight. It tells the audience what kind of story they are entering and why they should follow you.

Different stories call for different leads, but all strong leads share characteristics:

- clarity
- relevance
- precision
- purpose
- movement

Weak leads tend to be vague, overly general, cliché, or disconnected from the story's core.

Below are some main news lead types.

1. The Straight News Lead (Summary Lead)

This is the backbone of breaking news and urgent updates.
Purpose: deliver the essential facts immediately.
When to use: emergencies, announcements, policy changes, event recaps.

These leads work because they respect time and deliver impact quickly.

Weakness: rarely emotional or narrative.

2. The Scene Lead

One of the strongest tools for features, profiles, and narrative arcs.

Scene leads drop the reader directly into a specific moment, physical, emotional, or visual. They rely on sensory detail, character presence, and tension.

Scenes do not merely describe; they *activate* the story.

Example idea: "Two minutes before sunrise, Maria Alvarez stood barefoot on her porch, the eviction notice trembling in her hand."

A scene lead must be rooted in accurate reporting, not invented drama.

3. The Character Lead

This lead begins by anchoring the story in a compelling figure.

Used when the person *is* the entry point into the larger idea.

Works especially well for profiles and human-interest stories.

4. The Mystery or Tension Lead

Also called the "delayed reveal." It suggests something intriguing without giving away the point too soon.

Used sparingly, this technique can hook readers effectively but must avoid gimmicks.

5. The Thematic or Conceptual Lead

Useful for complex topics, investigations, or essays.
These leads introduce the big idea first, then bring in details or human anchors later.

Why Some Leads Fail

Leads often fall flat because they:

- start too broadly
- rely on cliché ("It was a day like no other…")
- bury the most interesting material
- overwhelm readers with data
- begin with generalizations instead of specifics
- lack movement or energy

A strong lead emerges when the reporter understands the story's *center.*

Scene Building: The Engine of Narrative Journalism

Scenes are the building blocks of storytelling. They bring reporting to life by showing, not just telling what happened.

A well-constructed scene includes:

- **setting** (time, place, sensory detail)
- **characters** (what they do, say, feel)
- **action** (movement, behavior, physicality)
- **purpose** (what the scene reveals about the larger story)

Scenes create emotional and intellectual connection. They also break up dense information and help readers visualize events.

However, scenes must always be:

- accurate
- verified
- grounded in reporting
- free of embellishment

> Students often mistake dramatization for detail. The rule is clear: *use only what you observed or verified.*

Pacing: Controlling the Reader's Attention

Pacing determines how quickly or slowly information unfolds.

Strong pacing uses variation:

- **fast pacing** for action, urgency, or simple facts
- **slow pacing** for emotional depth, complexity, or reflection
- **medium pacing** for background, transitions, and context

> Poor pacing feels monotonous, either breathless or sluggish. Good pacing feels intentional.

Examples of slowing down:

- detailed descriptions
- deeper character reflection
- quotes with emotional weight

Examples of speeding up:

- short declarative sentences
- compressed events
- quick scene summaries
- tight, precise language

Pacing should support the story's central tension.

Transitions: The Invisible Skill That Holds Stories Together

Transitions are one of the most underrated skills in journalism. They give stories coherence, clarity, and flow.

Transitions answer one key question: **"Why is this paragraph here, and why is the next one coming?"**

Strong transitions:

- connect ideas logically
- guide the reader through shifts in time, place, or perspective
- maintain narrative momentum
- signal changes in tone or focus

Types of transitions include:

1. Logical Transitions

Cause-and-effect, comparison, contradiction, expansion.

2. Temporal Transitions

"Later that afternoon…" "Two weeks earlier…" "By the time the meeting ended…"

3. Scene-to-Scene Transitions

Signaling physical movement or shifts in location.

4. Thematic Transitions

Linking ideas rather than events ("While Maria worried about eviction, her neighbors faced a different challenge…").

Weak transitions often rely on repetition, abrupt jumps, or unclear sequencing.

Techniques for Writing Complex or "Dry" Topics

Many stories reporters encounter feel dense: budgets, zoning laws, datasets, administrative processes. Structure helps, but narrative flow transforms these topics into accessible journalism.

Strategies include:

- using characters as entry points
- starting with a concrete example before moving into abstraction
- breaking complex concepts into digestible steps
- using active verbs and specific nouns
- replacing jargon with plain language
- pairing scenes with explanation
- using metaphors sparingly to clarify (not embellish)
- providing context exactly when readers need it

A budget story becomes compelling when readers see how one student can't afford required materials.

A zoning story matters when readers understand how it affects a corner store closing.

A policy story becomes alive when tied to a family navigating the process.

Bringing It All Together: Narrative Movement

Narrative flow is not just about transitions or scenes, it's about the *emotional and intellectual journey* of the reader. Movement exists when each paragraph builds on the last, creating momentum.

Movement requires:

- clarity of purpose
- strategic structure
- varied pacing
- purposeful scenes
- well-timed explanation
- thoughtful transitions
- a consistent center of gravity

> When movement works, the story feels inevitable: every detail belongs, every moment builds, every shift is earned.
>
> When movement fails, the story feels confusing or flat, even if the reporting is strong.

Light Checklist: Leads, Scenes & Flow

- Does the lead reflect the story's core purpose?
- Does each scene reveal new information or deepen meaning?
- Is pacing appropriate for the topic?
- Do transitions guide readers clearly?
- Is complex information broken into understandable segments?
- Does the story move with intention, not drift?

Reflection Activity

Choose a story you admire, news or a feature. Identify:

1. The lead it uses
2. How the first scene is constructed
3. Where pacing slows and where it speeds up
4. Three transitions that maintain flow
5. How the structure creates momentum

Write a one-page reflection on how these techniques shape your reading experience.

Section 6.3: Case Study Walkthrough & Structure Templates

Story structure becomes real when students see it applied to a full piece of reporting. In JOU 201, instructors often emphasize that the theories of inverted pyramids, hourglasses, and narrative arcs only gain meaning when writers understand how reporters actually decide what goes where. This section walks through a complete structural analysis of a feature story, showing how raw reporting transforms into a coherent narrative. It also provides simplified structure templates that students can use when drafting their own stories.

Case Study: Rebuilding After the Flood

Imagine a small town recovering from a sudden flood that destroyed dozens of homes and businesses. A student reporter is assigned to write a feature about a local barber, Mr. Alvarez, whose shop had been a gathering place for the community for over twenty years. The story has emotion, conflict, systemic issues, and strong character presence, exactly the kind of material that can be structured in multiple ways depending on the storytelling goals.

Step 1: Identifying the Story's Center

Before choosing a structure, the reporter needs clarity about the core of the story. Is it about the flood itself? The town's slow recovery? Insurance delays? Or the barber's personal resilience?

The strongest version focuses on Mr. Alvarez's journey while using his experience as a lens to show how recovery systems succeed or fail. This balance of individual narrative and community consequence gives the story depth and broader relevance.

Step 2: Choosing the Structure

Because the story contains both a newsworthy event and an emotional human arc, the hourglass structure is the strongest fit. It allows the reporter to open with essential facts about the flood, pivot into a narrative about Mr. Alvarez's experience, and close with the current status of recovery efforts.

Had the reporter chosen the inverted pyramid, the emotional arc would have disappeared. A full narrative approach might have worked, but the hourglass provides the right mix of information and storytelling.

Step 3: Building the Opening Scene

The reporter decides to open with a scene from the morning after the flood: Mr. Alvarez standing in front of his ruined shop, holding the soaked clippers he had owned since his first year in business. This moment is grounded in reporting—

it happened, it reveals character, and it symbolizes loss. The scene also leads naturally into the broader explanation of the flood's impact.

Step 4: Weaving in Context

After establishing the emotional foundation, the reporter adds the essential context: how much damage the flood caused, how many businesses were destroyed, how emergency management responded, and what challenges residents face. The context is placed here, not earlier, because readers are already anchored in a human moment and can now absorb the bigger picture without feeling overwhelmed.

Step 5: Developing the Narrative Middle

The story then shifts into a chronological sequence: the moment the water entered the shop, the evacuation, the loss of equipment, and the long wait for insurance processing. Each moment reveals both the character's emotional stakes and the systemic tensions behind the recovery process.

> Scenes are used sparingly but effectively: a neighbor helping salvage tools, a frustrating call with an insurance adjuster, an evening spent cleaning mud from family photographs. These details give the narrative movement.

Step 6: Returning to the Present

After the narrative sequence builds momentum, the story returns to the present. Mr. Alvarez has reopened in a temporary location, the town is still repairing streets, and community members are slowly rebuilding routines. The story ends not with a neat conclusion but with a sense of forward motion, readers leave with clarity about where things stand and what remains uncertain.

Why This Structure Works

The hourglass approach succeeds because it respects both the information needs of the audience and the emotional truth of the story. The factual top provides clarity, the narrative middle provides depth and connection, and the return to the present offers resolution without artificial closure. The structure allows readers to learn, feel, and understand at the same time.

Reflection on Structural Decision-Making

Students often assume structure emerges naturally while writing, but in reality, structure is a series of choices. In this case study, the reporter had to decide:

- which moment best opens the door for the reader
- when to bring in context
- how to pace emotional scenes with factual explanation
- which details deserve full scenes and which belong in summary
- where the story should end to feel honest and useful

These choices create rhythm and coherence. They turn raw reporting into narrative.

Simplified Structure Templates

Below are clean, narrative-friendly templates students can use when drafting.

Inverted Pyramid Template (News)

Begin with the most essential information, the five core questions. Follow with supporting details. End with background or secondary material. Keep the language direct and avoid unnecessary buildup.

Hourglass Template (Hybrid News + Story)

Open with essential facts to ground the reader. Then transition into a chronological narrative that explores the human dimension. Conclude by returning to the current status or broader implications.

Narrative Arc Template (Feature)

Start with a vivid scene or moment that introduces the central character or tension. Develop the story through rising action, complications, and emotional stakes.

Close with a reflective or forward-looking moment that conveys meaning without forced finality.

Profile Template (Portrait Writing)

Begin with a scene or moment that reveals something fundamental about the person. Provide background in a way that deepens, rather than interrupts, the portrait. Highlight contradictions, turning points, or defining traits. End on a note that reflects the theme rather than summarizing achievements.

Q&A Template (Interview-Centered Story)

Introduce the subject and why their voice matters. Present the conversation in clean, chronological flow. Provide brief transitions only where necessary to maintain context.

Reflection Activity

Choose a real news event or feature idea you might write about. Draft two short outlines: one using an inverted pyramid and one using a narrative arc. Write a paragraph reflecting on how the tone, emphasis, and reader experience would differ depending on the structure.

FOLLOWING A STORY TO RESOLUTION

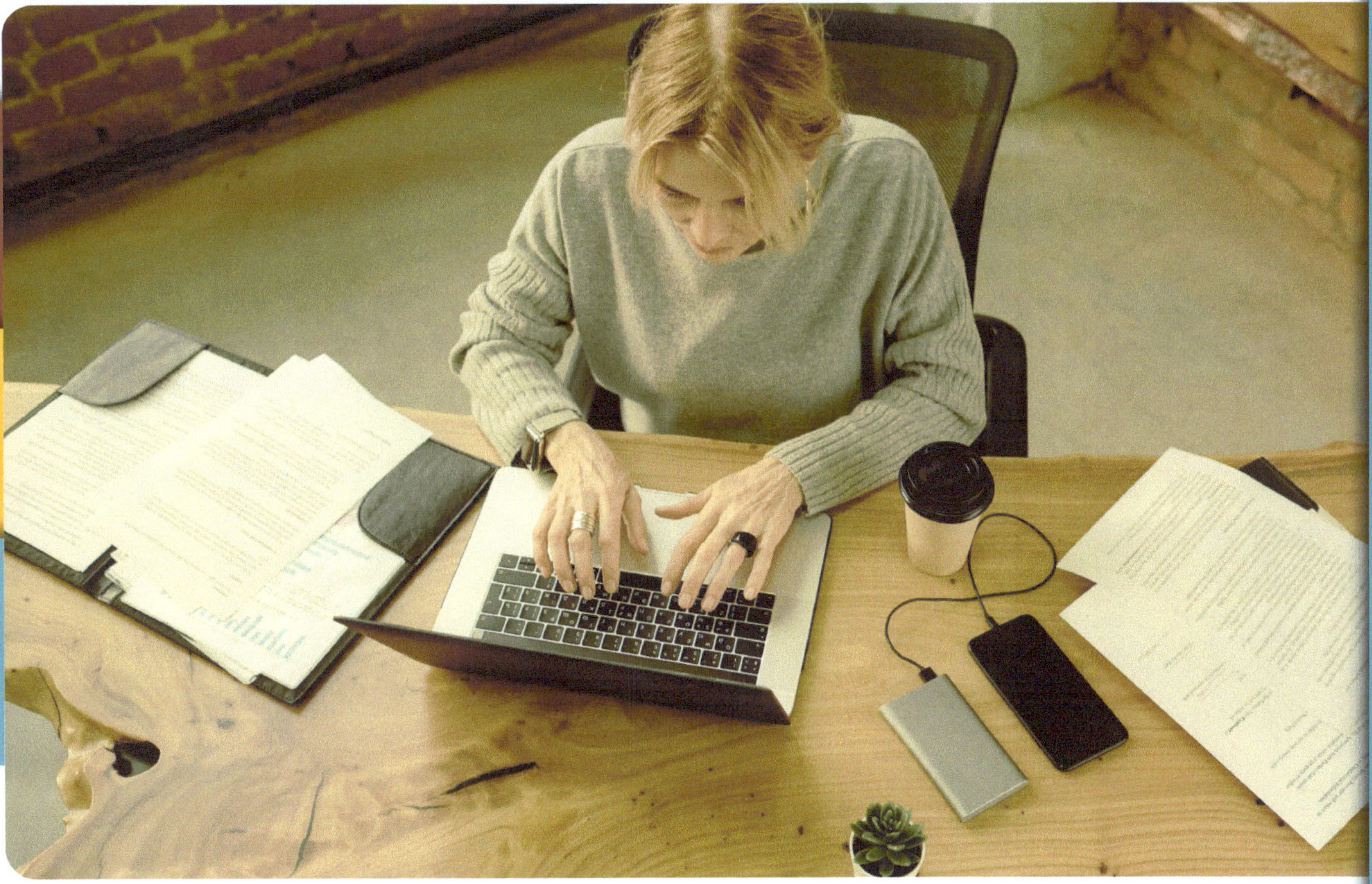

PLACED-BASED LEARNING SERIES

Overview

News reporting does not happen in a single moment. Most important stories unfold over time, sometimes days, sometimes months, sometimes years. They evolve as new facts emerge, as institutions respond, as communities react, and as consequences ripple outward in ways no reporter can predict on day one. This chapter introduces students to the practice of *following a story*, a central skill in professional journalism that demands persistence, clarity, ethical discipline, and strategic thinking. It is one of the most challenging and rewarding parts of the craft.

Good reporters know that ongoing stories require more than simply "keeping up." They require reporters to track developments, verify new claims, revisit sources, and communicate updates in ways that maintain coherence for the audience. When a story evolves across multiple days or multiple news cycles, the danger is losing readers to confusion—too many details too fast, too many contradictions, too much noise. The journalist's role is to organize this movement, to maintain clarity even while the story shifts beneath their feet.

Following a story also tests a reporter's ethical grounding. Every new lead carries the temptation to speculate, to assume, or to publish before facts are ready. Incomplete information, conflicting accounts, emotionally charged moments, and institutional silence all create uncertainty. Ethical journalism requires patience: the discipline to verify, the willingness to wait, and the ability to communicate what is known, what is unknown, and what is still unfolding. In rapidly developing stories, legal cases, policy debates, public safety incidents, campus crises, this is not easy. But it is precisely where credibility is built.

This chapter explores the full spectrum of following an ongoing story. It begins with the practical work of covering courts, policies, and investigations, showing students how to track incremental updates without overwhelming or confusing readers. It then examines the ethical challenges of following leads, what to do when tips are unverified, when sources contradict each other, or when information comes faster than confirmation. The chapter also dives into the realities of multi-day news cycles, where deadlines are constant, details change rapidly, and the pressure to publish increases.

A major focus is on handling uncertainty. Students will learn how to write clearly while acknowledging what is still unknown, how to organize facts when the story is in motion, and how to avoid the common pitfalls that lead to errors in breaking news. Verification becomes even more critical during crises: confirming quotes, double-checking official statements, and being transparent about what is still unfolding. A detailed case study later in the chapter walks through the process of covering a rapidly developing crisis, demonstrating how reporters make decisions hour by hour, update by update, while protecting accuracy and fairness.

By the end of this chapter, learners will understand that following a story is not simply extending a single article, it is a discipline. It requires strong judgment, clear communication, and the ability to remain steady when information is shifting and incomplete. Whether covering a court case, a policy battle, a protest, a public health emergency, or a breaking investigation, journalists must follow the story with patience, humility, and a commitment to truth. This is how reporters earn trust—not by being fast, but by being consistently responsible.

Section 7.1: Covering Ongoing Stories: Courts, Policies & Investigations

Ongoing stories are the backbone of daily journalism. They demand endurance, judgment, and an ability to guide the audience through events that shift, stretch, and evolve over time. Unlike feature stories, which offer a more controlled environment—ongoing coverage requires reporters to enter a moving stream and keep their footing even when the current changes direction without warning. This type of reporting forms the heart of journalism, where students learn how to interpret long-term developments, maintain narrative clarity, and remain accountable to the facts as they emerge.

Following an ongoing story means the journalist is responsible for telling a public narrative that is not yet complete. Every update must add understanding rather than noise. Every new development, no matter how small, must be placed in context. Readers must be able to step into the story at multiple points and still feel oriented, informed, and respected. This requires the reporter to be both a witness and an interpreter, someone who gathers new information while also remembering the story's roots. Often, journalists rely on the "nut graf" to catch readers up quickly.

Every update must add understanding rather than noise. Every new development, no matter how small, must be placed in context.

What Is a Nut Graf?

In journalism, a **nut graf** (short for "nutshell paragraph") is the paragraph, usually placed high in a story, that tells readers **what the story is really about and why it matters**. While the lead captures attention, the nut graf provides the essential context, focus, and significance that guide the rest of the article.

A strong nut graf typically does three things:

1. **Explains the central point or theme** of the story in clear, concise terms.
2. **Shows why the story is important right now**, often connecting individual events to a broader issue, trend, or consequence.
3. **Provides the roadmap** for what readers can expect as they continue through the article.

> In other words, the nut graf is where the journalist makes a promise to the reader: *Here is the heart of the story and why you should keep reading.* It transforms a compelling lead into a cohesive narrative by grounding the reporting in purpose, relevance, and clarity.

Ongoing stories often unfold in public institutions, courtrooms, legislative chambers, city council meetings, police departments, administrative agencies, where processes move slowly and the stakes are high. Journalists must learn not only how to extract news from these environments but also how to explain them. Many readers have never entered a courtroom or observed a policy hearing. They rely on journalists to bridge that gap and make procedural steps understandable without losing accuracy.

More importantly, ongoing stories test a reporter's discipline. New rumors emerge. Conflicting accounts circulate. Officials sometimes release partial statements. Witnesses may change details or recall events differently weeks later. In these moments, the journalist must resist the temptation to speculate or publish prematurely. Instead, they must choose patience, precision, and context. The reporter covering an ongoing story becomes a stabilizing force, someone who helps the community distinguish between real developments and unverified noise.

This section examines three major arenas where ongoing stories unfold, **courts, policies, and investigations**, and teaches students how to navigate them responsibly, ethically, and with professional clarity.

Courts: Reporting in a Slow but High-Stakes Environment

Courtrooms move with a rhythm that new journalists often misunderstand. To the untrained eye, proceedings can appear slow, repetitive, procedural, or even anticlimactic. But a journalist who follows a court story over weeks or months learns that a single case contains dozens of small moments that collectively determine its outcome. Many of these moments happen quietly: a judge's scheduling decision, a legal motion filed by one side, a brief exchange between attorneys, a witness who hesitates, or a document entered into evidence.

Covering courts requires patience and presence. Reporters must attend hearings that seem minor because they often contain clues about what is coming next. A defense attorney's shift in tone may hint at a new strategy. A prosecutor's request for additional time may signal upcoming evidence. A judge's comments, even ones that do not result in immediate rulings, may reveal skepticism or concern.

A journalist following a court story should maintain a running timeline: every motion, ruling, hearing, delay, and procedural action. This living timeline becomes the spine of the coverage. Readers depend on the journalist to track the case accurately, especially when it spans months or when multiple charges or defendants are involved.

A journalist following a court story should maintain a running timeline: every motion, ruling, hearing, delay, and procedural action.

Court reporting also tests clarity. Legal terminology is dense, and the journalist must translate it into accessible language without diluting its meaning. A reporter must explain what a suppression hearing actually is, what "probable cause" requires, how discovery works, and why a judge grants a continuance. These explanations appear simple, but they require accuracy, confidence, and a deep understanding of the system.

Above all, court reporting demands fairness. It is easy to focus only on dramatic testimony or emotional reactions. But responsible journalism also includes procedural moments that readers may not initially see as news. By explaining these stages, the journalist helps the public understand how justice unfolds, not in dramatic bursts, but in careful increments.

Policy Coverage: Understanding Decisions That Shape Communities

While court stories revolve around cases, policy stories revolve around ideas, proposed, debated, amended, approved, implemented, and evaluated. Policy reporting is an ongoing narrative of power, negotiation, and community consequence. It requires the journalist to follow legislative calendars, committee meetings, draft proposals, public hearings, and stakeholder responses.

Policy stories often begin with a simple question: *What problem is this policy trying to solve?* But the coverage that follows requires far more work. Policies evolve slowly, and the journalist must guide readers through the evolution without losing them in technical language. This means identifying the decision points: when a proposal is introduced, when amendments are added, when public opposition emerges, when costs become clearer, when lawmakers shift their positions, and when the issue reaches a vote.

> A strong reporter approaches policy as a story rather than as a document. They describe how the policy came to be, who is affected, who opposes it, what evidence supports it, and what motivations drive stakeholders. Policies are rarely neutral, there are values embedded in every choice, and journalism must help reveal them.

Policy reporting also requires the journalist to balance detail and accessibility. Too much legislative jargon overwhelms readers; too little detail misrepresents the complexity. The reporter must distill without flattening, simplify without distorting.

Each update must reinforce the larger narrative arc: how this policy evolved, where it stands now, and what remains uncertain.

Investigations: When the Story Grows with Every Call

Investigative stories represent the highest degree of ongoing reporting because they are shaped by the journalist's own work rather than by scheduled events. Every interview, document, or tip has the potential to change the direction of the story. One lead may contradict another. A source may reveal a new allegation. A public records request may uncover information that shifts the timeline or expands the scope of the issue.

Every interview, document, or tip has the potential to change the direction of the story.

Following an investigative story requires deep organization. A reporter must maintain meticulous notes, labeled files, source logs, interview transcripts, summaries of conflicting accounts, and collections of documents. Without organization, an investigative story collapses under its own weight.

Investigations also test ethical judgment. Not every allegation should be published the moment the reporter hears it. Some tips lead nowhere. Some sources distrust each other. Some documents reveal sensitive information that must be handled carefully. The reporter must verify each piece of information thoroughly, often from multiple sources, before presenting it to the public.

In investigations, patience becomes a form of responsibility. Rushing leads to errors—errors that harm individuals and undermine trust. Reporters must read deeply, interview repeatedly, corroborate claims, and fact-check aggressively. New journalists sometimes imagine investigations as dramatic breakthroughs, but in reality, they unfold slowly through dozens of discreet decisions.

Tracking Updates Without Losing the Story's Shape

Ongoing stories often generate a flood of details that can confuse readers if not handled carefully. A strong journalist acts as a guide, not simply presenting information, but organizing it. This requires the reporter to maintain a clear sense of the overarching narrative: where the story began, what the stakes are, who the central actors are, and what the unresolved questions include.

Each update becomes an opportunity to reinforce coherence. The journalist must contextualize developments without repeating entire histories. A brief, well-placed recap, or a single sentence connecting the new update to earlier events, helps readers stay oriented. If the reader loses their sense of direction, the story loses its ability to inform.

Following a story also requires the journalist to avoid tunnel vision. When reporting day after day, it is easy to become so immersed in the details that the larger significance becomes blurry. Stepping back, reviewing the timeline, revisiting the central issues, and remembering the broader community implications is essential.

it is easy to become so immersed in the details that the larger significance becomes blurry.

Ethical Responsibilities While Returning to Sources

Ongoing coverage often requires the reporter to speak with the same sources repeatedly. Over time, relationships form, sometimes cooperative, sometimes tense. The journalist must balance persistence with respect, understanding that sources may feel fatigue, anxiety, or pressure from sustained public attention.

Ethical source management includes:

- being transparent about what will be published
- clarifying background/off-the-record terms each time

- acknowledging emotional strain
- respecting boundaries
- avoiding dependence on a single source

A long-term story requires structural fairness: no single voice should dominate coverage simply because they answer calls more quickly. The journalist must seek out new perspectives and avoid letting convenience shape representation.

Clarity as a Form of Public Service

Following a story is ultimately an act of service to the community. Each update helps the public understand systems that are often opaque: the court's logic, the government's reasoning, the investigative process. Clarity becomes a public good. It empowers citizens to participate meaningfully in civic life, whether by attending meetings, responding to proposals, advocating for changes, or simply understanding how the news affects their daily lives.

A journalist who can maintain clarity across a series of updates provides stability to the public conversation. They help people see developments not as chaotic, isolated events but as connected, meaningful parts of a larger whole.

A journalist who can maintain clarity across a series of updates provides stability to the public conversation.

Reflection Activity

Identify an ongoing issue in your community, such as a public safety case, a local development conflict, a school board controversy, or a new policy proposal. Create a detailed timeline of events so far. Then write two paragraphs: one explaining how the story began, and another summarizing the latest development. Compare the paragraphs. Ask yourself: How does the update depend on the history? What information must be carried forward for the story to remain coherent?

Section 7.2: Following Leads Ethically & Handling Multi-Day News Cycles

Following a story through multiple news cycles is one of the most demanding tasks in journalism. Unlike a single-day assignment, multi-day stories require reporters to manage uncertainty, shifting information, conflicting accounts, and relentless deadlines. The journalist becomes a long-distance runner, not just gathering facts, but maintaining clarity and discipline throughout a process that may last days, weeks, or even months. The heart of this work lies in ethical lead-tracking and in managing the pressure of an evolving narrative without sacrificing accuracy.

Multi-day reporting demands a heightened level of awareness: the reporter must remember what the audience knows, what they don't know, and what the reporter is still working to verify. They must keep detailed notes, timelines, and working theories while maintaining enough humility to revise those theories when new information overturns earlier assumptions. This is where journalism intersects with judgment. A lead may appear promising but prove unreliable. A source may sound confident but be misinformed. A rumor may spread quickly online but collapse under verification. The journalist's responsibility is to remain calm, methodical, and ethical even as the story accelerates around them.

The Nature of Leads: Tips, Signals & Unverified Possibilities

Every ongoing story is shaped by leads, pieces of information that suggest, hint, or point toward something that may (or may not) become part of the public narrative. Leads are not facts. They are starting points. But beginners often confuse leads with confirmed information, rushing to publish before the lead is tested. This is where professional discipline matters.

Leads can come from anywhere: a witness, a public official, a social media post, a leaked document, an overheard conversation, a community rumor, or a sudden development in court. Some leads are solid and quickly verifiable; others are fragile and must be handled with caution. Treating all leads with equal weight is irresponsible. An ethical journalist must categorize them intuitively:

- Which leads have supporting evidence?
- Which leads are mere speculation?
- Which leads require immediate follow-up?
- Which leads require waiting?
- Which leads carry risk if published prematurely?

Newsrooms often teach reporters to treat leads as signals, something that may guide their next phone call, next document request, next question in a press conference. A lead is not the story; it is only the invitation to begin searching.

Ethical Boundaries: What It Means to "Follow" Without Assuming

The ethical challenge in following leads is striking a balance between exploration and restraint. Reporters must pursue leads aggressively but publish only what is confirmed. This is especially difficult in emotionally charged or high-pressure stories, where the public demands immediate answers and speculation spreads rapidly.

Ethical lead-tracking requires the journalist to constantly ask:

- *Do I have enough verification to report this?*
- *Am I implying more certainty than the evidence supports?*
- *Am I giving the audience clarity, or am I feeding confusion?*
- *Is someone's reputation or safety at risk if I publish too early?*
- *Does this detail belong in the public conversation yet?*

In some cases, pursuing a lead ethically means telling the audience that something is "unverified" or "under investigation." Transparency protects credibility. When journalists hide uncertainty, they lose public trust; when they explain uncertainty, they gain respect.

The Pressure of Multi-Day News Cycles

A multi-day news cycle is not simply a story that lasts a long time. It is a cycle in which new developments emerge regularly, each one demanding rapid attention. These may involve:

- new statements from officials
- updated information from authorities
- new witnesses stepping forward
- documents becoming available
- public reactions or protests
- policy responses
- legal filings
- social media speculation

The reporter must monitor all these developments without becoming overwhelmed. Multi-day reporting has a rhythm: early confusion, partial clarity, contradicting narratives, institutional responses, public debates, and eventual resolution. Each phase requires different reporting strategies.

For example, the first day may be dominated by uncertainty. The second day may focus on sorting facts from misinformation. The third day may highlight victims, impacts, or institutional accountability. The fourth day may shift toward long-term consequences, policy implications, or broader analysis.

A strong journalist adapts to each stage and never assumes that early information will remain true. Early reporting is often contradictory. The journalist's role is to update without distorting, correct without hiding mistakes, and maintain a clear timeline so the audience understands how information evolved.

Managing Conflicting Information Without Losing Credibility

One of the hardest parts of multi-day reporting is dealing with conflicting accounts. A witness may contradict another witness. An early police statement may clash with later evidence. Officials may revise timelines. Social media may distort facts. In these moments, inexperienced reporters feel pressure to "pick a version" of the story and stick with it. But professionals resist that impulse.

Conflicting information is not a sign of journalistic failure, it is a natural part of evolving news. The journalist's responsibility is not to pretend the contradictions don't exist. Instead, they must acknowledge them openly and explain what is known, what is unclear, and why accounts differ.

> A sentence like, *"Authorities initially said X, but newly released documents indicate Y, raising questions about Z,"* provides clarity while maintaining transparency. This approach helps the audience understand not only the facts but also the uncertainty surrounding them.

The Role of Verification in a Fast-Moving Story

Verification becomes even more important during multi-day cycles because the cost of error increases dramatically. A mistake made early in the story can echo for days, shaping public perception and damaging credibility long after corrections are issued. That is why reporters must verify every new detail before publishing—even when the pressure is intense.

Verification involves:

- checking statements against official documents
- cross-checking witness accounts
- confirming details with multiple sources

- reviewing public records
- comparing institutional statements for discrepancies
- contacting experts for clarification

Breaking news is where verification is most difficult, but also where it matters most. Reporters must learn to work quickly but carefully, maintaining accuracy even in the face of chaos.

Sustaining Narrative Coherence Across Multiple Updates

A story that unfolds over many days can easily lose its shape. Details pile up. New actors enter. Old details fade from memory. Readers skim updates without understanding their relationship to earlier coverage. A skilled journalist must keep the narrative intact, gently re-orienting the audience with every new piece of information.

Readers skim updates without understanding their relationship to earlier coverage.

This coherence is maintained through:

- strategic re-summaries
- clean transitions
- clear explanations of significance
- consistent framing
- a steady tone that avoids dramatization

Each update is both a standalone report and a piece of a larger narrative. The journalist becomes the caretaker of continuity.

The Emotional Dimension of Multi-Day Reporting

Long-running stories often involve trauma, conflict, loss, and uncertainty. Reporters must interact repeatedly with people who are grieving, frightened, angry, or overwhelmed. The emotional weight can be heavy and managing emotional fatigue is a professional responsibility.

This means:

- maintaining empathy without losing objectivity
- taking breaks when necessary
- protecting one's mental well-being
- understanding the emotional burden placed on sources
- approaching people repeatedly with sensitivity

Multi-day reporting is not just logistical; it is emotional labor.

When Leads Collapse: The Discipline to Pivot

Not every lead becomes part of the story. Some leads fall apart. Others turn out to be misunderstandings. Some contradict high-quality information. The journalist must be willing to pivot, sometimes abandoning a line of inquiry they spent considerable time pursuing. This is not wasted effort, every dead-end teaches the reporter something about the story and helps narrow the scope.

The journalist must be willing to pivot, sometimes abandoning a line of inquiry they spent considerable time pursuing.

> The reporter's humility is tested when a promising lead collapses. But the strongest journalists do not cling to incorrect assumptions; they adjust and move forward.

Reflection Activity

Choose a news story that unfolded over several days—such as a protest, public safety incident, political dispute, court hearing, or policy controversy. Write a brief analysis explaining how the story changed between Day 1 and Day 5. Identify moments where journalists had to revise earlier reports or navigate conflicting information.

Section 7.3: Uncertainty, Verification in Breaking News & Covering a Rapidly Developing Crisis

Breaking news rarely arrives in a neat, understandable package. It comes suddenly, unevenly, and often in fragments that contradict one another. In the earliest minutes and hours of a crisis, there is confusion, speculation, emotional reactions, and an overwhelming amount of partial information. This uncertainty is not a flaw of reporting; it is the natural environment that breaking news creates. A journalist covering such events must learn to operate inside uncertainty, rather than trying to eliminate it prematurely. This is where real professionalism begins.

When a crisis unfolds, the public desperately craves answers. People want to know what has happened, whether they are safe, how many people are affected, and what the consequences might be. But at the exact same moment, reliable information is scarce. Authorities may not have the full picture yet. Witnesses may recall events differently. Social media may amplify rumors as though they were fact. It is in this volatile space that the journalist must remain calm, disciplined, and methodical.

Understanding Uncertainty as a Working Condition

Uncertainty is not temporary; in many breaking news cases, it continues for several hours or even days. The journalist's role is to acknowledge uncertainty without letting it dominate the narrative. This means being clear with readers about what is known, what remains under investigation, and what early reports cannot yet confirm. Doing so builds trust. Readers quickly learn they can rely on the journalist for measured, accurate updates, not dramatic assumptions or sensationalism.

Uncertainty also requires humility. A reporter must accept that he or she will not know everything immediately. They must tolerate the discomfort of incomplete knowledge without rushing to fill the gaps with speculation or unverified claims. This discipline is one of the hallmarks of professional reporting.

Verification Under Pressure

Verification during breaking news is its own specialized skill. It requires speed, but also caution. The reporter must gather information quickly but resist the temptation to publish prematurely. Every piece of information, whether from officials, witnesses, documents, or digital sources, must be tested against other evidence.

During a fast-moving event, verification often focuses on a few essential questions: Can this detail be confirmed? If yes, how? If not, why not? Even when information appears reliable, professional reporters pause long enough to ask whether they are interpreting it correctly or adding unintended assumptions.

Although lists should be used sparingly, here a small one is genuinely helpful. The most common sources of early information in a crisis include:

- **Eyewitness accounts**, which are vivid but often incomplete or contradictory.
- **Official statements**, which provide authority but may be partial or preliminary.
- **Social media posts**, which spread quickly but often contain exaggeration or guesswork.

These are not inherently unreliable; they simply require confirmation. A journalist must be prepared to check multiple angles before committing any detail to publication.

One of the core principles in breaking news verification is that the more urgent a claim seems, the more carefully it must be checked. Highly emotional or dramatic information is often the most unstable. Professional journalists learn that restraint is not a delay, it is protection.

Writing Cleanly Even as Facts Shift

As new information arrives, the narrative will inevitably evolve. A responsible journalist must write updates that are clear, calm, and anchored in confirmed facts. They should avoid language that oversells or implies certainty prematurely. For example, words like "appeared," "reportedly," or "unconfirmed" have specific uses, when applied correctly, they signal transparency; when overused or misused, they create confusion.

One of the hardest tasks is maintaining coherence between updates. Readers may encounter the story at different points in time, so the journalist must organize each update in a way that connects new facts to the larger timeline. This requires careful attention to chronology and significance: what happened first, what changed later, and why each development matters.

A well-written update also distinguishes between what is newly confirmed and what earlier information has been corrected or clarified. Rather than hiding errors or quietly removing outdated details, ethical journalists acknowledge evolution openly. This strengthens reader trust, especially during chaotic events.

Emotional Pressure & The Responsibility to Stay Measured

Breaking news places emotional pressure on everyone: the public, the authorities, the people directly involved, and the journalists themselves. Reporters may feel adrenaline, fear, urgency, empathy, or frustration. But they must learn to work through these emotions without letting them influence the accuracy or tone of the story.

This emotional discipline is crucial for several reasons. First, heightened emotion can make speculation feel more tempting. Second, emotional writing can distort information, making the situation appear more catastrophic or more resolved than it actually is. Third, sources in crisis situations may be traumatized or overwhelmed, requiring extra sensitivity and care.

Students often underestimate how emotionally draining breaking news reporting can be. It requires stamina, not just physical, but mental. The journalist must remain aware of their own reactions, pace themselves, and avoid letting urgency become panic. The public depends on journalists to stay centered during moments when the community feels destabilized.

Case Study: A Rapidly Developing Campus Crisis

Consider a scenario on a university campus where a loud noise triggers emergency alerts. Students flee buildings. Social media becomes chaotic with claims ranging from "explosion" to "active threat." Rumors multiply, and the entire campus community grows anxious within minutes.

Hour 1: Confusion and Fragmented Information

During the first hour, the journalist gathers direct observations and credible statements. Emergency vehicles are visible. Students report hearing a loud noise. Some describe smoke in the distance; others insist they saw nothing unusual. Authorities have not yet given any explanation.

At this stage, the journalist publishes only what is confirmed: the location, the presence of responders, the evacuation procedures, and the fact that officials have not yet identified the cause. They avoid labeling the event as an explosion or accident. They avoid implying intent. They avoid drawing conclusions from partial witness accounts. This restraint prevents misinformation from escalating.

Hour 2: First Official Clarifications

Authorities provide an initial statement: a small mechanical malfunction in a maintenance area caused a loud release of pressure. There is no ongoing threat. The journalist updates the story clearly and calmly, explaining how the new information reframes what the public saw and heard.

Hour 3–5: Sorting Rumors from Evidence

Online speculation now expands, with students sharing screenshots that imply intentional harm. The journalist checks each claim but publishes none until authorities confirm or deny them. During this period, the journalist interviews maintenance staff, requests incident reports, checks building schematics, and documents the timeline of events in detail.

Hour 6: Final Confirmation

Eventually, the fire department releases a technical report confirming the mechanical malfunction. The journalist provides a comprehensive final update that synthesizes the entire timeline, clarifies misinterpretations, corrects earlier assumptions, and offers information about follow-up actions.

By the end of the evening, the story is clear, accurate, and responsibly sequenced, because the journalist maintained discipline during the most uncertain moments.

Pitfalls in Crisis Coverage

Even experienced reporters make mistakes during fast-moving events. The most common pitfalls include jumping to conclusions based on eyewitness emotion, relying too heavily on social media chatter, overstating the level of threat, and failing to follow up when early information changes. Another frequent error is cluttering updates with too much detail, overwhelming readers rather than guiding them.

A disciplined journalist must continually return to three core questions when writing breaking news:

- What is truly confirmed right now?
- What still needs verification?
- What has changed since the last update?

These questions act as an internal compass.

Checklist for Responsible Crisis Reporting

A journalist in a breaking event should always ask:

- "What do we know for certain?"
- "What do we believe but cannot yet confirm?"
- "How did we verify each element we plan to publish?"

These few questions, asked consistently, prevent the majority of avoidable errors.

Reflection Exercise

Choose any major breaking-news event from your region and find the first three news stories written about it. Compare how the narrative changed between each update. Then identify one moment where uncertainty played a major role and explain how the journalists handled, communicated, or struggled with that uncertainty.

CHAPTER 8

MEDIA LAW, EDITING & ETHICAL DECISION-MAKING

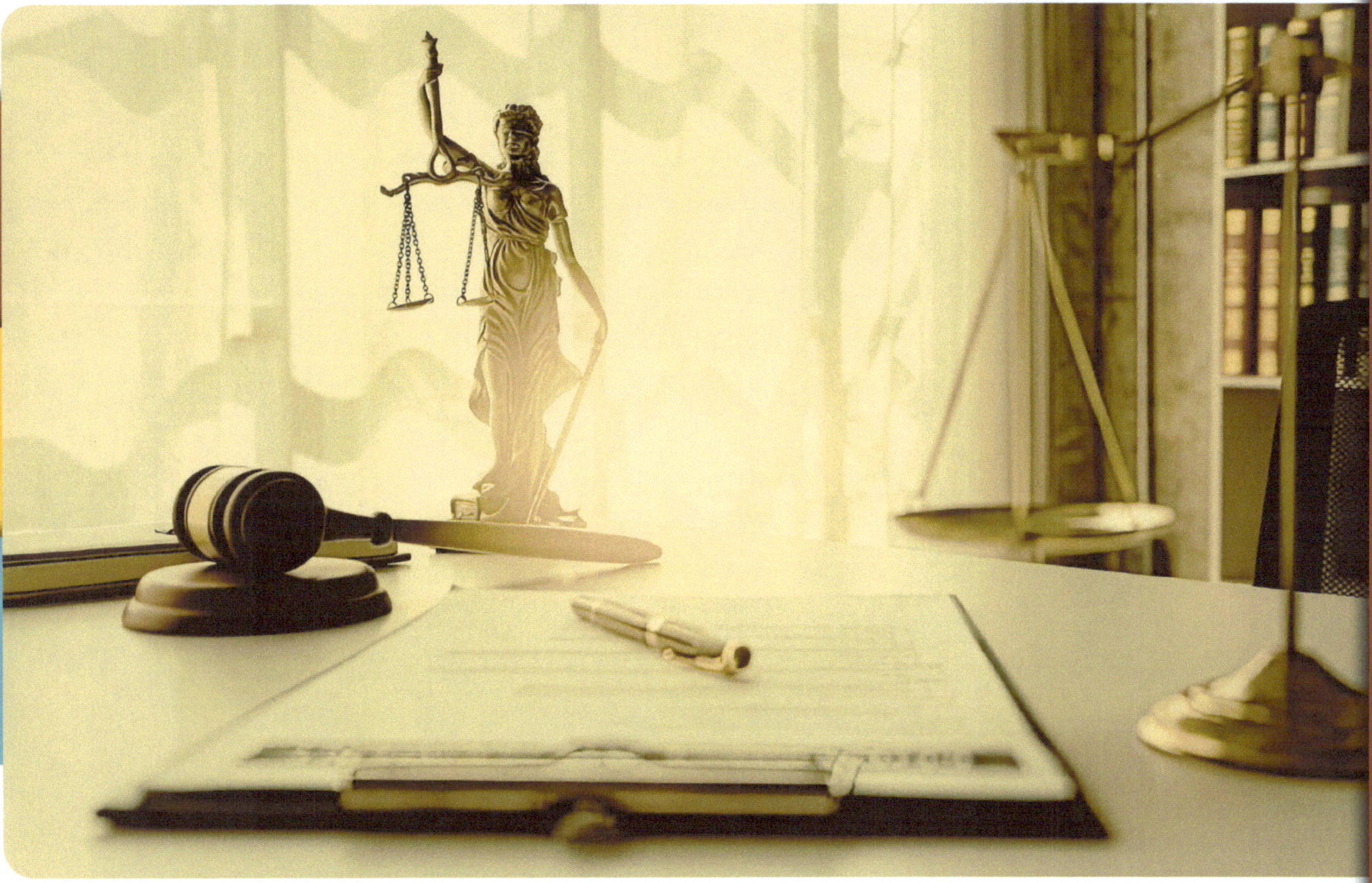

PLACED-BASED LEARNING SERIES

Overview

Journalism is built on three intertwined forces: **law**, **editing**, and **ethics**. Each of these forces plays a distinct role, yet none can stand independently. Legal literacy protects journalists from liability and ensures that published information respects the rights of individuals. Editing protects the story from distortion, error, unfairness, and misrepresentation. Ethical decision-making protects communities, especially vulnerable ones, from harm, exploitation, or inaccurate portrayals. Together, they form the backbone of professional responsibility in journalism.

This chapter brings together the most advanced skills students have been developing across the entire course: finding stories, interviewing, verifying, following developing narratives, representing communities with nuance, and writing with clarity. Chapter 8 asks students to move from *craft* to *judgment*. It challenges them to think like editors—individuals who must anticipate consequences, make decisions that protect the truth, and ensure that journalism upholds public trust.

The work that happens in the editing stage is rarely visible to the public, yet it is the stage with the most impact on fairness and accuracy. A single edit can shift meaning, tone, or cultural framing. A headline can protect a vulnerable person or expose them. A misplaced phrase can suggest guilt where none exists. In this sense, editing is not merely a technical skill but an ethical one. Reporters must constantly balance clarity with caution, precision with accessibility, and speed with responsibility.

Media law provides the guardrails for this work. Understanding defamation, privacy, intrusion, copyright, and public records laws allows journalists to report confidently and ethically. Law does not restrict good journalism; it empowers it. When students recognize what the law protects, they gain the ability to publish boldly yet responsibly.

Finally, ethical decision-making ensures that journalism remains grounded in humanity. Coverage of trauma, conflict, marginalized communities, and culturally complex regions requires empathy, humility, and awareness. Lessons from APP 101, especially the importance of avoiding stereotypes and harmful cultural framing, shape the way journalists approach communities like Appalachia, immigrant groups, rural populations, or any community historically misrepresented by the media.

Throughout this chapter, learners will explore the editor's role, the legal responsibilities of journalists, and the ethical decisions that shape a story long before it reaches the public. A final case study challenges students to apply everything they've learned, analysis, verification, cultural awareness, legal literacy, and ethical reasoning, to a nuanced real-world dilemma. The chapter closes with a capstone reflection that ties all eight chapters together, showing how responsible journalism is not a series of disconnected tasks, but a continuous discipline guided by clarity, fairness, accountability, and respect.

This is the final chapter of the course not because it ends the work of journalism, but because it marks the point where students transition from learners to practitioners, ready to engage the world with skill, conscience, and intention.

Section 8.1: The Editor's Role in Modern Journalism

Editing is the quiet engine of journalism. It is the stage where stories gain clarity, where fairness is restored, where accuracy is strengthened, and where the public trust is either protected or eroded. Reporters often work closest to the ground, interviewing, observing, gathering documents, and navigating emotionally charged situations, but editors shape how that work enters the public sphere. Their responsibility is not simply technical; it is conceptual, ethical, cultural, and legal. The editor carries a duty that extends far beyond correcting grammar or improving sentences. They are custodians of truth, community perception, and newsroom integrity.

Editors occupy a unique vantage point. While reporters see the story through proximity, editors see it through distance. That distance does not mean detachment, it means perspective. An editor must imagine how a community will interpret the story, how sources will be represented, how readers will respond, and how the piece may interact with long-standing cultural narratives or legal constraints. The goal is to protect not just the text, but the people inside it and the audience receiving it. Good editing transforms reporting into journalism.

An editor must imagine how a community will interpret the story, how sources will be represented, how readers will respond, and how the piece may interact with long-standing cultural narratives or legal constraints

Understanding the Editor's Mindset

Editing begins with a mindset shaped by curiosity, skepticism, compassion, and responsibility. Editors must read with their eyes on several levels at once: What does the story say? What does it imply? What does it leave out? How will it sound to someone who knows nothing about the topic? How will it sound to someone who knows too much? How will it affect the people being written about?

An editor constantly anticipates confusion and corrects it. They look for leaps in logic, unexplained transitions, or emotional overstatements. They identify places where the reporter has assumed reader knowledge or unintentionally framed someone through bias. This awareness forms the foundation of editorial judgment.

Editors also practice what is sometimes called *constructive distance*. Because they are not as close to the story as the reporter, they can identify inconsistencies more easily. This distance allows them to read as a public would read, not with the insider knowledge of a reporter, but with the genuine curiosity and vulnerability of an informed citizen trying to understand an event or community.

Editors also practice what is sometimes called ***constructive distance*****.**

In this way, editors play the role of surrogate reader, verifying whether every sentence serves clarity, fairness, accuracy, and nuance.

Editing for Clarity, Fairness & Accuracy

Clarity is the first signal of respect for readers. A story may contain important information, but if it is confusing, jargon-filled, or structured poorly, its usefulness evaporates. Editors reshape stories so readers can follow them without struggling to interpret meaning. This requires attention to pacing, transitions, context, and the balance between narrative and information.

Fairness, however, is the editor's deeper responsibility. Fairness means ensuring that people are represented with appropriate context, that their statements are not distorted by selective quotation, and that the story does not lean on dramatic or sensational details at the expense of accuracy. A story about a neighborhood conflict, for example, may unintentionally exaggerate the intensity of tensions if the writer focuses heavily on the loudest voices. Editors restructure such stories to bring proportionality. They ensure that quieter voices, often the most vulnerable or marginalized, are not overshadowed by the most assertive or politically connected sources.

Accuracy is the anchor of this work. Editors double-check timelines, confirm spellings, scrutinize quoted material, and review the logic of causal statements. Something as small as a misplaced clause can unintentionally accuse someone of wrongdoing. A quote without context can mislead readers. A rushed summary can strip a story of nuance. Editors protect against these mistakes by carefully examining how meaning emerges sentence by sentence.

Accuracy and fairness are not merely editorial preferences; they are forms of accountability. They ensure that journalism remains trustworthy.

Something as small as a misplaced clause can unintentionally accuse someone of wrongdoing.

Recognizing Stereotypes & Responsible Cultural Framing

One of the editor's most sensitive responsibilities involves cultural framing. Stories about communities, especially rural regions, low-income neighborhoods, immigrant families, or historically misrepresented groups, carry a legacy of stereotypes. Places like Appalachia have been shaped in the public imagination not by lived reality, but by decades of reductive narratives: poverty, backwardness, homogeneity. These narratives persist because they are easy to repeat and hard to dismantle.

Editors must learn to spot these patterns as they emerge in drafts. A sentence that mentions a single struggling family might unintentionally imply that an entire community is defined by hardship. A detail about addiction might reinforce a stereotype of a region plagued by dysfunction. Even word choice—"isolated," "forgotten," "impoverished", carries weight. Editors must ask whether these words reflect reality or simply echo familiar tropes.

Cultural framing also applies to urban communities, immigrant groups, religious minorities, LGBTQ+ populations, and other groups often represented through the lens of conflict, crisis, or vulnerability. Editors examine whether the story emphasizes problems without offering context about strengths. They question whether people are portrayed with agency or as passive symbols. They ensure that complexity replaces caricature.

Responsible cultural framing requires not just awareness but intentionality. It demands that editors understand how stories travel, how they shape public perception, influence policy, and either reinforce or challenge long-standing assumptions.

Editing as Legal Protection: Defamation, Privacy & Copyright

Editors are often the newsroom's legal buffer. While reporters focus on gathering truth, editors must consider how that truth is presented. A story that is factually accurate can still be legally risky if it is framed carelessly.

Defamation occurs when false statements harm someone's reputation. But editors know defamation risk also comes from implication. A sentence that places an individual near wrongdoing without clarifying their role may lead readers to assume guilt. Editors must catch these subtleties. They ensure that allegations are clearly attributed, that facts are not exaggerated, and that opinion is not mistaken for proven information.

Privacy concerns arise when a story includes personal details that are not essential to public understanding. Even if information is accurate, editors consider whether publishing it violates dignity or causes unnecessary harm, particularly when dealing with minors, trauma survivors, or private citizens. Editors balance public interest with human sensitivity.

Copyright issues emerge when images, documents, or materials created by others are used without permission. Editors review whether fair-use standards apply, whether content has been transformed sufficiently, and whether attribution is clear. Their vigilance prevents costly legal disputes and protects the newsroom's credibility.

> Media law is not simply a technical requirement; it is another layer of ethical decision-making. Editing with legal awareness ensures the story is strong enough to stand up in public, in court, and in history.

Ethical Pressure Points in Editorial Decision-Making

Ethical dilemmas often surface during editing, not reporting. A reporter may include a dramatic detail about a victim's background, unaware that it reinforces harmful narratives. They may quote an official without checking whether the statement is misleading. They may publish a detail that is accurate but unnecessarily invasive.

Editors must navigate these dilemmas carefully. They ask whether a detail adds value or simply adds heat. They consider whether a story is shaped by empathy or voyeurism. They question whether the reporter's emotional proximity has clouded their judgment.

Ethical editing requires the courage to remove material, even powerful material, if it risks harming individuals or communities. It also requires the confidence to ask reporters for more context, deeper nuance, or additional voices. Ethical editing is a form of care. It protects the integrity of journalism and the dignity of people involved.

Illustrative Example: When Editing Determines the Whole Story

Imagine a reporter covering a series of overdoses in a small rural community. Their draft opens with vivid descriptions of abandoned houses and a quote from a resident who says the town is "dying." While the details are true, the overall framing echoes long-standing stereotypes about rural decline. The story, as written, risks portraying the community as helpless and broken.

An experienced editor steps in.

They ask the reporter to include context: the town's economic transition, community recovery programs, families supporting one another, and structural challenges that extend beyond the region's control. They remove overly dramatic visuals that sensationalize suffering and add interviews with people working on solutions. The focus shifts from "a dying town" to "a community navigating crisis with resilience."

In this example, editing transforms the narrative, from deficit framing to responsible representation. The story becomes deeper, more accurate, and less harmful. It also becomes more useful to the community.

They remove overly dramatic visuals that sensationalize suffering and add interviews with people working on solutions.

Common Editorial Pitfalls

Even skilled editors must remain vigilant. Common pitfalls include:

- relying too heavily on reporter assumptions
- leaving in ambiguous phrases that imply wrongdoing
- failing to challenge dramatic but misleading framing
- over-editing and erasing the reporter's voice
- under-editing and allowing harmful details to remain

> Avoiding these pitfalls requires awareness, humility, and a commitment to continuous learning.

Reflection Exercise

Find a published news article about a vulnerable community, rural, low-income, immigrant, or otherwise marginalized. Identify three places where editing could have improved cultural framing, strengthened accuracy, or reduced harm. Rewrite those sections with adjustments that reflect fairness, nuance, and responsible representation.

Section 8.2: Revising for Clarity, Fairness, Accuracy & Harm Reduction

Revision is the deep work of journalism, the slow, deliberate process that transforms reporting into responsible storytelling. While writing captures the first version of events, revision is where the story becomes ethically grounded, legally sound, culturally aware, and accessible to readers. Revision is taught not as an optional polish but as a moral obligation. It is where the journalist steps back from the adrenaline of reporting and asks: *Does this story tell the truth clearly? Does it treat people fairly? Does it avoid unnecessary harm? Does it stand up to legal scrutiny?* Revision is where the real discipline begins.

Revision is taught not as an optional polish but as a moral obligation.

Reporters often approach stories with passion and urgency, especially when the subject is emotionally charged or fast-moving. But passion alone can distort meaning. Without careful revision, a story may emphasize the dramatic over the essential or simplify a complex social issue into a digestible but misleading narrative. The editor's task in revision is to pull the story back into alignment: to ensure that insight outweighs sensation, that complexity outweighs stereotype, and that facts outweigh assumptions.

Revision for **clarity** is the first step, because clarity determines whether readers can make sense of the information at all. A story may contain accurate facts yet still confuse the reader, if the writer assumes too much reader knowledge or jumps too quickly between ideas. Editors look for these gaps and bridge them. They refine transitions, smooth pacing, and restructure paragraphs so that the narrative follows a logical arc. Clarity also requires eliminating jargon, defining unfamiliar terms, and ensuring that the story's central point remains visible throughout. In revision, clarity becomes a form of respect: respect for the reader's time, attention, and need for understanding.

Clarity also requires eliminating jargon, defining unfamiliar terms, and ensuring that the story's central point remains visible throughout.

Fairness is the next pillar. A story can be factually correct yet still unfair if it frames people or communities inaccurately. Reporters may unintentionally rely on the most dramatic quotes or focus heavily on conflict while ignoring quieter but equally important perspectives. Fair revision requires the editor to ask: *Does this story give each side the context needed? Are some voices being amplified because they are easier to access rather than because they contribute meaningfully? Does the structure skew interpretation?* Fairness involves adjusting emphasis, balancing viewpoints, and sometimes asking the reporter to return for additional interviews to fill gaps.

Fairness is also cultural. Regions like Appalachia, and many other communities historically misrepresented by the press, are vulnerable to oversimplification. A single phrase like "forgotten community" or "struggling region" may carry decades of stereotype. Editors learn to sense those patterns instantly, recognizing where the language reinforces tropes instead of reflecting reality. They revise such stories by adding nuance, seeking additional voices, and widening the frame to include structural explanations rather than leaving readers with reductive cultural assumptions.

Revision for **accuracy** goes far beyond checking names and dates. It requires verifying that meaning has not been distorted in the writing process. A statistic without context can mislead. A quote placed at the beginning of a paragraph may imply causation that was never intended. Editors analyze how readers will interpret each detail, not just whether the detail is technically correct. Accuracy also includes ensuring that timelines are coherent, that quotes are attributed correctly, and that no sentence suggests more certainty than the evidence supports. This is where reporters' notes, transcripts, and recordings become crucial. Revision restores fidelity between the text and the original reporting.

But the heart of Section 8.2 lies in harm reduction, an area where editing becomes not just an intellectual process but an ethical one. Harm occurs in journalism when individuals or communities are exposed, misrepresented, or stigmatized unnecessarily. Sometimes this harm emerges from revealing sensitive personal details that have no public-interest value. Other times, it emerges subtly through framing: portraying a community as helpless, depicting a group through their problems rather than their humanity, or repeating familiar stereotypes that shape public perception long after the story ends.

Harm occurs in journalism when individuals or communities are exposed, misrepresented, or stigmatized unnecessarily.

Harm reduction requires editors to imagine how a person in the story might feel reading the published version. It requires sensitivity toward trauma, poverty, immigration status, disability, and cultural identity. It requires editors to question whether a story exploits pain for emotional effect, whether it includes details that could endanger someone's safety, or whether the story's tone reinforces negative assumptions about a place or people. Harm reduction also extends to protecting minors, survivors of violence, and individuals facing public scrutiny, groups who often bear the heaviest consequences of journalistic disclosure.

Legal considerations intertwine with harm reduction. A story that accidentally implies criminal wrongdoing can expose the newsroom to defamation claims. Revealing private information, medical records, addresses, family details—may violate privacy laws. Using copyrighted images or materials without permission may lead to legal complications. Trained and experienced editors learn to catch these issues during revision. They adjust ambiguous phrasing, remove unnecessary identifiers, ensure all information meets public-interest standards, and confirm that copyrighted materials are used in compliance with fair-use guidelines.

Revision also benefits from structured practice. In advanced editing courses, students often receive flawed drafts filled with subtle biases, incomplete context, or legally risky statements. Their goal is not simply to correct the surface but to diagnose deeper issues, implicit stereotypes, missing voices, skewed framing, or narrative imbalance. Through these exercises, students learn to see stories the way seasoned editors do: with analytical distance, cultural sensitivity, and legal awareness.

The depth of revision becomes clearer through example. Imagine a reporter writes a story about a food pantry in a low-income neighborhood. Their draft highlights dramatic quotes about hardship, describes the area using terms associated with "danger" or "decline," and features images of people waiting in long lines. While the facts may be true, the framing reinforces a narrative of helplessness. An editor revising this story would step back and ask: *Is this representation fair? Does it capture the community's complexity? Does it rely too heavily on problems without acknowledging resilience?* The editor might add context about economic conditions, include interviews with families who contribute to community-building, or shift the emphasis from desperation to structural challenges. Through revision, the story becomes more accurate and more humane.

> Revision is where journalism confronts its responsibilities directly. It is where editors ensure that the story does not simply inform but informs ethically, fairly, and with full awareness of its impact. Good revision honors the truth not only in what it says, but in how it says it.

Section 8.3: Legal Responsibilities, Ethical Dilemmas & Full-Course Wrap-Up

Journalism relies not only on curiosity and craft, but on a deep understanding of the responsibilities that come with publishing information. Laws, ethics, and editorial judgment form the invisible framework that protects both the journalist and the people being written about. The work of journalism is not complete when the reporting ends; rather, it enters its most delicate stage. This is where legal risks must be assessed, ethical dilemmas must be resolved, and the story must be positioned in a way that reflects truth without causing unnecessary harm. Section 8.3 expands these ideas by exploring how legal responsibilities and ethical complexities converge in real newsroom decision-making, and how all the skills built throughout this book come together in practice.

Journalism's power to uncover wrongdoing or reveal uncomfortable truths is inseparable from its ability to inflict damage when misused. A single sentence can shape public perception. A misplaced detail can affect a life. A poorly attributed claim can create legal liability. Because of this, the final stage of editorial work demands maturity, restraint, and an unwavering commitment to fairness. This section prepares students to navigate the most challenging aspects of the profession: balancing the public's right to know with individual dignity, distinguishing verified facts from speculation, and applying a legal and ethical filter to every editorial decision.

A misplaced detail can affect a life. A poorly attributed claim can create legal liability.

Understanding Legal Boundaries in Journalism

Media law is not a separate universe; it is woven into every editorial choice a journalist makes. The legal standards governing defamation, privacy, and copyright shape what can be said, how it can be said, and which details require protection.

Editors must be familiar with these boundaries because they often recognize legal problems long before reporters do.

Defamation is among the most misunderstood areas for emerging journalists. It is not limited to outrageous falsehoods; subtle implications can be equally dangerous. A sentence that places someone near wrongdoing without clarifying their involvement may invite readers to assume guilt. Even the placement of a quote can suggest causal relationships that were never proven. Editors must examine whether accusations are clearly attributed, whether facts support each interpretive leap, and whether the narrative could be read as implying misconduct in a way that goes beyond the evidence. This level of scrutiny is essential in stories about crime, public officials, or allegations of misconduct.

Privacy presents another significant concern. Publishing a fact that is technically true does not make it ethically or legally sound. Individuals who are not public figures have a reasonable expectation of privacy, especially when dealing with medical conditions, financial troubles, family matters, or trauma. Editors must determine what serves legitimate public interest and what crosses into exploitation or voyeurism. This line becomes especially sensitive when minors or vulnerable individuals are involved. A detail that seems small in a draft can have profound consequences once published.

Copyright raises its own complications in the digital era. Images, videos, and written materials circulate widely online, tempting journalists to incorporate them into stories without proper clearance. Editors must evaluate whether a piece of content qualifies for fair use, whether it has been transformed sufficiently in the reporting process, and whether the source has been correctly credited. Failure to do so can expose a newsroom to lawsuits or reputational damage.

> These legal concerns are not technical obstacles; they are foundational protections. They ensure that journalism remains credible and that the people being reported on are treated with respect.

Ethical Complexities That Shape Editorial Choices

While law defines what must not be done, ethics shape what ought not to be done. Ethical dilemmas emerge where legal standards leave room for interpretation. A story may be publishable, yet still harmful. A detail may be accurate but unnecessary. Editors must navigate these gray areas with sensitivity and foresight.

A story may be publishable, yet still harmful. A detail may be accurate but unnecessary. Editors must navigate these gray areas with sensitivity and foresight.

One of the most challenging ethical issues arises when reporting on trauma. Stories involving violence, sudden loss, illness, or public crises require a delicate balance. Reporters may encounter individuals in distress who reveal intimate details without understanding the long-term implications of publication. Editors must protect these individuals, even when they have given consent, by assessing whether inclusion of those details serves the story or merely intensifies its emotional impact. Ethical journalism prioritizes dignity over drama.

Ethics also governs the portrayal of communities. Many communities—rural regions, immigrant neighborhoods, low-income families—are frequently framed through reductionist narratives. Journalists not trained in cultural competencies can unintentionally reinforce stereotypes by focusing on deficits, dramatizing hardship, or ignoring structural factors that shape people's lives. Editors must challenge these patterns during the revision process. They must examine whether the draft relies on clichés, whether it unfairly highlights a sensational detail, or whether it neglects the complexity of real lives. Ethical editing means presenting communities as full human environments, not as symbolic representations of problems.

Another ethical pressure emerges when covering conflict or controversy. Journalists may feel that "both sides" must be presented equally, even when one side is grounded in misinformation. Editors must distinguish between balance and accuracy, ensuring that the desire for fairness does not distort the truth. This requires confidence and clarity, an understanding that ethical journalism is not neutral but responsible.

Cultural Framing, Stereotypes & Representational Consequences

Stories do not exist in isolation; they exist within broader cultural narratives. Editors must recognize the historical and social contexts that shape how readers interpret stories. The framing of a community, its struggles, its achievements, its people—shapes public understanding far beyond the specific event being reported.

Representational harm is subtle but powerful. A story that depicts an Appalachian town as economically devastated without acknowledging resilience reinforces a narrative of helplessness. A story that focuses exclusively on crime in an immigrant neighborhood may unintentionally strengthen fear-based stereotypes. Even the choice of adjectives, "troubled," "forgotten," "isolated", can convey an unintentional verdict about a community's worth.

Editors must become experts at reading beyond the literal text. They examine whether a story frames people as agents or objects, as stereotypes or individuals. They ask whether the narrative explains structural challenges or simply attributes outcomes to cultural flaws. They question whether the story's tone aligns with reality or echoes long-standing biases.

> Cultural framing is not a cosmetic concern; it is a core part of responsible journalism.

Editorial Decision-Making Under Pressure

The hardest editorial decisions happen under pressure: tight deadlines, intense public attention, competing interests, emotional environments. Breaking news intensifies these pressures, leaving little time for reflection.

Editors must remain grounded in uncertainty, especially when information is incomplete. They must resist the temptation to publish unverified claims simply because they are circulating widely. They must encourage reporters to pause, verify, and question assumptions even when social media demands instant answers.

Sometimes the pressure comes from within the newsroom. A reporter who has invested significant effort in a story may resist edits that reduce emotional intensity or remove powerful scenes. Editors must navigate these professional tensions with diplomacy and authority. Their duty is not to appease but to protect the integrity of the story.

Other times, the pressure comes from external forces, public officials, community leaders, or powerful institutions seeking to influence the narrative. Editors must maintain independence, ensuring that coverage reflects verified truth rather than political pressure.

Editors must maintain independence, ensuring that coverage reflects verified truth rather than political pressure.

In all situations, editorial decision-making requires a steady hand, a clear mind, and a strong ethical compass.

Case Study: When Law, Ethics & Culture Collide

A reporter investigates a cluster of illnesses in a rural farming community. Local residents believe a nearby factory is contaminating the water supply. Social media amplifies fears. Advocacy groups begin issuing statements. The factory denies all responsibility. The community is caught between suspicion and fear.

The reporter gathers interviews, documents, and observations, then submits a draft suggesting that the factory's waste practices are likely causing the contamination. While the draft includes emotional interviews and dramatic scenes, the evidence remains circumstantial. Scientific testing is incomplete. Government agencies have not issued findings.

The editor intervenes.

They must balance:

- the **community's legitimate fear**
- the **public's right to know**
- the **legal risk of implying negligence**
- the **ethical duty to avoid fueling panic**
- the **historical pattern of rural communities being portrayed as powerless victims**

The editor revises the story by:

- removing language that suggests causation
- clarifying what authorities know and what they do not
- adding context about environmental history in the region
- including expert voices explaining the difference between correlation and proof
- shifting the narrative from blame to investigation
- adding details about community resilience and local organizing efforts

The final story is balanced, responsible, and legally sound—not because the reporter lacked skill, but because the editor provided essential guidance.

This example demonstrates how editing becomes the anchor of professional judgment.

Common Pitfalls in High-Stakes Editing

Even experienced editors encounter recurring challenges:

- letting emotional storytelling overshadow accuracy
- relying on dramatic anecdotes instead of structural context
- failing to distinguish between rumor and verified fact
- unintentionally reinforcing community stereotypes
- allowing powerful sources to control the narrative
- removing so much detail that the story loses depth
- failing to remove details that unnecessarily expose private individuals

Awareness of these pitfalls strengthens editorial intuition.

Final Reflection: What It Means to Be a Journalist

Journalism is not just a profession; it is a public trust. It requires courage, humility, discipline, and empathy. It demands that journalists tell the truth—but also that they understand the consequences of how they tell it. Good journalists do not chase perfection. They chase responsibility. They understand that every story is an opportunity to illuminate rather than exploit, to clarify rather than confuse, to dignify rather than diminish.

The final message of this course is simple: **Journalism is an act of service. Do it with honesty, with care, and with your whole conscience.**

GLOSSARY OF TERMS

News Values

Impact

The degree to which a story affects people's lives is measured not only by how many people are affected, but by how deeply their lives are changed. Impact can be immediate or long-term, visible or structural, and often intersects with systems such as education, health, economics, or policy.

Why it matters: Impact determines urgency. It helps journalists prioritize stories that meaningfully shape people's lived realities rather than those that are simply interesting.

Timeliness

The relevance of a story to the present moment or unfolding events. Timeliness is not only about speed, but about recognizing when information becomes meaningful—when something changes, escalates, or demands public attention.

Why it matters: News gains value when it reflects what is happening now, but responsible journalism balances speed with accuracy.

Proximity

The closeness of a story to the audience's lived experience geographically, culturally, or emotionally. Proximity includes not only physical distance, but shared identity, values, or circumstances that make a story feel personally relevant.

Why it matters: People are more likely to engage with stories that feel connected to their own lives, communities, or concerns.

Prominence

The involvement of influential individuals, institutions, or systems in a story. This includes elected officials, public figures, corporate leaders, and organizations with decision-making power.

Why it matters: Power increases public attention because the actions of prominent actors often have wide-reaching consequences.

Conflict

Tension created by competing needs, pressures, interests, or systems. Conflict in journalism is not limited to disagreement—it can emerge from structural inequities, policy decisions, resource allocation, or unresolved community issues.

Why it matters: Conflict reveals stakes and helps audiences understand what is at risk, who is affected, and why the story matters.

Novelty

The unusual, unexpected, or surprising aspect of a story. Novelty can draw attention by highlighting what is different from the norm, but it must be handled carefully to avoid distortion or sensationalism.

Why it matters: Novelty captures attention, but responsible journalists ensure that what is unusual is also meaningful and contextualized.

Human Interest

Story elements that evoke empathy, curiosity, or emotional connection through personal experience. Human interest often centers on individuals navigating broader issues, making complex topics more accessible.

Why it matters: It helps audiences connect to the story, but must be used ethically to avoid exploitation or oversimplification.

Ethics

Verification

The process of confirming information through evidence, multiple sources, documentation, and cross-checking. Verification is an ongoing discipline, not a single step, and includes evaluating credibility, corroborating claims, and identifying uncertainty.

Why it matters: It separates journalism from rumor, opinion, and misinformation.

Transparency

Showing audiences how information was gathered, what is known, and what remains uncertain. Transparency includes explaining sourcing decisions, acknowledging limitations, and correcting errors openly.

Why it matters: It builds trust by allowing audiences to understand the reporting process.

Independence

Freedom from influence—political, financial, personal, or social—that could shape reporting unfairly. Independence requires maintaining professional boundaries and avoiding conflicts of interest.

Why it matters: It protects credibility and ensures journalism serves the public, not external pressures.

Accountability

The obligation to take responsibility for reporting decisions, correct errors, and engage with audiences when mistakes occur. Accountability is an ongoing commitment to ethical practice.

Why it matters: Trust is built not through perfection, but through responsibility and transparency.

Minimize Harm

An ethical principle requiring journalists to consider the potential impact of their reporting on individuals, communities, and vulnerable populations. This includes avoiding unnecessary intrusion, stereotyping, or retraumatization.

Why it matters: Journalism has real-world consequences, and ethical reporting balances truth-telling with care.

Defamation and Media Law

Defamation

False statements presented as fact that harm a person's reputation. Defamation law distinguishes between opinion and fact and requires journalists to understand both legal standards and ethical responsibilities.

Why it matters: It is one of the most common legal risks in journalism and can result in significant consequences for both individuals and news organizations.

Libel

Defamation that appears in written or published form, including print, digital, and visual media.

Why it matters: Most journalism is published, making libel the most relevant form of defamation for reporters.

Slander

Defamation that is spoken, typically in broadcast or verbal communication.

Why it matters: Applies to radio, television, podcasts, and live reporting environments.

Actual Malice

A legal standard established in New York Times Co. v. Sullivan requiring proof that a statement was published with knowledge of its falsity or with reckless disregard for the truth.

Why it matters: It protects press freedom by setting a high bar for public officials and figures to prove defamation.

Narrative Theory

Character

A real person whose experiences and perspective help reveal the meaning of a story. In journalism, characters are not fictional constructs but individuals whose lives intersect with broader issues.

Why it matters: Characters make complex topics understandable and emotionally resonant.

Stakes

What a person, group, or community stands to gain or lose within a story. Stakes may be economic, social, emotional, or political, and often operate at multiple levels simultaneously.

Why it matters: Stakes create urgency and clarify why the story matters.

Narrative Arc

The progression of a story through movement and development, often involving a beginning, rising tension, and some form of clarity or outcome. In journalism, this arc reflects reality rather than a constructed plot.

Why it matters: Structure helps audiences follow complex information and retain meaning.

Resolution (Journalism)

Clarity about where a story stands at a given moment—not a forced or artificial ending. Journalism often documents ongoing issues rather than complete conclusions.

Why it matters: Journalism reflects reality, which is often unresolved and evolving.

Media Trust

Public Trust

The audience's belief that journalism is accurate, fair, and reliable. Trust is built over time through consistent ethical practice, transparency, and accountability.

Why it matters: Without trust, journalism cannot effectively inform or engage the public.

Credibility

The perceived reliability and authority of a journalist or news organization. Credibility is shaped by accuracy, consistency, expertise, and ethical behavior.

Why it matters: It influences whether audiences believe and act on information.

Local Journalism Impact

Place-Based Journalism

Reporting rooted in the culture, history, relationships, and lived realities of a specific community. It prioritizes local knowledge, context, and sustained engagement over outsider perspectives.

Why it matters: Context leads to more accurate, relevant, and trusted reporting.

Narrative Equity

The fair, accurate, and complete representation of communities in storytelling. Narrative equity challenges stereotypes and ensures that stories reflect the full complexity of people's lives.

Why it matters: Stories shape how communities are perceived—and how resources and opportunities are distributed.

News Desert

A community with little or no access to consistent, reliable local news coverage. News deserts often result from economic decline in media and can leave communities without essential information.

Why it matters: Lack of access to local news weakens civic participation, accountability, and democratic function.

ABOUT THE AUTHOR:

Dr. Melissa Newman is a journalist, author, fundraiser, and civic engagement strategist whose work examines how story shapes power, policy, and local economies. She is also the creator of the News Media & Civic Engagement Place-Based Learning Series©, an intensive training program designed for non-journalists who want to begin working in their local newsrooms. The curriculum is currently part of a pilot program with Press Forward Blue Grass and Report for America, with plans for national scaling.

Grounded in her roots in Kentucky journalism and decades of leadership in philanthropy, fundraising, and education, Melissa works at the intersection of reporting, resource mobilization, and systems change. She believes that the way communities are represented in local news directly influences public trust, philanthropic investment, workforce development, and long-term opportunity, and that when local journalism is weakened, entire civic ecosystems suffer.

She has raised and stewarded millions of dollars for place-based initiatives and has helped newsrooms, nonprofits, and cross-sector partnerships build the financial and civic infrastructure needed to sustain local storytelling.

Her writing and research focus on poverty, media representation, and narrative equity, with particular attention to how strong local news ecosystems drive democratic participation, economic vitality, and community resilience. She frequently speaks nationally about rebuilding trust in local journalism and positioning news as essential civic and economic infrastructure.

Her message is both simple and urgent: story is everything. When communities control their narratives—and when local news is strong enough to carry those stories forward—we don't just change perception. We change investment, policy, and what is possible for generations to come.

www.ingramcontent.com/pod-product-compliance
Lightning Source LLC
LaVergne TN
LVHW070121110826
845147LV00002B/165

* 9 7 8 1 6 2 5 5 3 1 1 7 9 *